BY Pearl S. Buck

CHINA PAST AND PRESENT

ONCE UPON A CHRISTMAS

CHINA AS I SEE IT

TO MY DAUGHTERS, WITH LOVE

FOR SPACIOUS SKIES
    [with Theodore F. Harris]

THE GIFTS THEY BRING
    [with Gweneth T. Zarfoss]

THE JOY OF CHILDREN

FRIEND TO FRIEND
    [with Carlos P. Romulo]

MY SEVERAL WORLDS

THE CHILD WHO NEVER GREW

AMERICAN ARGUMENT

TALK ABOUT RUSSIA

WHAT AMERICA MEANS TO ME

OF MEN AND WOMEN

HOW IT HAPPENS

TELL THE PEOPLE

AMERICAN UNITY AND ASIA

FIGHTING ANGEL

THE EXILE

THE CHINESE NOVEL [NOBEL PRIZE LECTURE]

THE GODDESS ABIDES

MANDALA

THE THREE DAUGHTERS
    OF MADAME LIANG

THE GOOD DEED

THE NEW YEAR

THE TIME IS NOON

DEATH IN THE CASTLE

THE LIVING REED

FOURTEEN STORIES

COMMAND THE MORNING

LETTER FROM PEKING

COME MY BELOVED

IMPERIAL WOMAN

THE HIDDEN FLOWER

GOD'S MEN

PAVILION OF WOMEN

KINFOLK

FAR AND NEAR

PEONY

VOICES IN THE HOUSE

BRIGHT PROCESSION

PORTRAIT OF A MARRIAGE

THE PROMISE

DRAGON SEED

TODAY AND FOREVER

OTHER GODS

THE PATRIOT

THIS PROUD HEART

A HOUSE DIVIDED

THE MOTHER

THE FIRST WIFE AND OTHER STORIES

SONS

THE GOOD EARTH

EAST WIND: WEST WIND

THE TOWNSMAN

THE LONG LOVE

THE ANGRY WIFE

ALL MEN ARE BROTHERS [SHUI HU CHUAN] translated from the Chinese

CHINA
PAST AND
PRESENT

Pearl S. Buck

CHINA PAST AND PRESENT

WITH PHOTOGRAPHS FROM MAGNUM BY

Henri Cartier-Bresson   Rene Burri

Hiroshi Hamaya

Marc Riboud   Helen Snow

THE JOHN DAY COMPANY

New York

Photographs from Magnum by
Rene Burri: pages 11, 35, 51, 53, 57, 63, 79, 91, 95, 153, 175
Henri Cartier-Bresson: pages 5, 25, 29, 39, 43, 103, 109, 131, 139, 145, 149
Hiroshi Hamaya: page 17
Marc Riboud: pages 7, 47, 55, 67, 73, 77, 83, 87, 99, 113, 121, 125, 127, 135, 159, 165
Helen Snow: page 45

Poem on page 69 reprinted from *Science and Civilization in China* by Joseph Needham, by permission of Cambridge University Press, as quoted in *The Soul of China* by Amaury de Riencourt.

Excerpt on page 118 reprinted by permission of *The Christian Science Monitor* from "A visitor looks at education in China" by Charles Mossop, from the April 22, 1972 issue of *The Christian Science Monitor*. Copyright © The Christian Science Publishing Society. All rights reserved.

Excerpt on pages 129–32 reprinted by permission of G. P. Putnam's Sons from *The Revenge of Heaven* by Ken Ling. Copyright © 1972 by Dr. Ivan London and Miriam London.

Excerpt on Page 136 reprinted by permission of Coward, McCann and Geoghegan, Inc. from *The Soul of China* by Amaury de Riencourt. Copyright © 1958 by Amaury de Riencourt.

Copyright © 1972 by Creativity, Inc.

All rights reserved. No part of this book may be reprinted, or reproduced or utilized in any form or by any electronic, mechanical or other means, now known or hereafter invented, including photocopying and recording, or in any information storage and retrieval system, without permission in writing from the Publisher.

The John Day Company, 257 Park Avenue South, New York, N.Y. 10010
An Intext Publisher

Published on the same day in Canada by Longman Canada Limited.

Printed in the United States of America

Library of Congress Cataloging in Publication Data
Buck, Pearl (Sydenstricker) 1892–
    China past and present.
    Includes bibliographical references.
    I. Title.
PS3503.U198Z536   818'.5'203   [B]   72-6121

CHINA
PAST AND
PRESENT

I

My earliest memories are of the people of China. My first memory is of a kindly Chinese face, a woman's face, not young, but symbolizing to me both love and authority. It is the face of my Chinese nurse. The face is no longer young because my nurse was nurse also to my two sisters and my brother, who died in early childhood before I was born. It is my Chinese nurse whose forefinger I clasped when I took my first steps. Always precocious, I began to walk when I was six months old. I know because I remember—or think I remember. It is indeed exasperating to have a memory that begins too young and continues too long. I know, because this is my memory. It goes back too far, it holds everything too fast, it does not forget anything— a relentless, merciless, disobedient memory, for there are some things I would like to forget. But I never forget. Therefore I remember struggling to walk when I should have been content to sit upright and play with my toys. At least that is what Wang Amah used to tell me, pretending to scold me in her loving fashion.

"You!" she cried. "You, making yourself walk when you should have been willing to be a baby! You nearly pulled off this forefinger! It is longer than the others."

She showed me the forefinger. At three I examined it with scientific care. "It is not longer," I said.

She shook the finger at me. "You were born in the Year of the Dragon. It is not good for a girl to be born in a Year of the Dragon. What will you do next?"

The answer to this often-asked question varied with my mood and my ambition of the moment. But I am not important. She is the one I remember, my dear old Chinese nurse. An American friend, who also grew up in China, has a theory that we China-bred people love or hate the people of China depending upon whether our Chinese amahs were kind and lovable or unkind. If we loved them, we love the Chinese people and China. If we did not experience that early love, we did not develop it later. It may be so. Certainly in my case the plenteous love poured out upon me by Wang Amah aroused in me an answering love for her people. My American friend was not as fortunate. His nurse was young and less patient and he does not love China—at least not as I do.

Yet Wang Amah could be and always was firm with me. She never punished me. She did not believe in punishment. Instead she exhorted me. These exhortations could be and often were long. They began with her request that I sit down in my chair. How well I remember that little chair! It was made of bamboo and was therefore light enough for me to move to the spot she designated.

While she exhorted, she darned our family stockings or clothes—usually mine, for I was an inveterate tree climber, partly for mercenary reasons since my mother paid me twenty Chinese cents for every crow's nest I could dismember, providing it had not reached the stage of eggs or small birds. This activity resulted in a full mending basket for Wang Amah. Thus engaged, she educated me in proper behavior, feminine lore, her family history, Chinese history in general as she had learned it from the experience of her long life.

Such history was vivid indeed. It covered the last three quarters of a century of the Ch'ing Dynasty in which she had been born and in the last decade of which I was born. She described for me in exciting detail the fearful T'ai P'ing Rebellion, a Chinese rebellion against the Manchu government under which we lived. The leader of this was a Chinese named Hung, who gathered about him other rebels whose purpose was to overthrow the throne in Peking and set up a Chinese Dynasty. The Manchu ruler at the time was the famous—and infamous—Tzu Hsi, who had risen from being an Imperial concubine to being herself the Empress.

The dynasty, however, had for years been in slow decline. Taking advantage of this fact, Hung had organized his rebellion. Like most Chinese events, it was dramatic. Hung had been the son of a well-to-do peasant. He was given an education, however, and like all young men who were educated, he went up for the Imperial Examinations, hoping to get a job in the Civil Service. Only a man with education and brains could pass the examinations. This insured getting the country's best men into the government, an attainment unique to the Chinese. It was a great loss when, in the revolutionary years, the Imperial Examinations were abolished and politics took their place.

Unfortunately, Hung failed the examinations, although he went up for them three times. By chance, as he left the third time in deep despondency to return to his country home, a man stood at the gate handing out small tracts. He took several of these carelessly and, when he reached home, put them away with all his books, resigned to a farmer's life.

One rainy day, after seven years of such a life, he took out his books in melancholy memory. There were the tracts, and he read them. They were translations of the Christian gospels. He read and was fired and inspired. Was not Jesus the son of a humble carpenter? Yet he rose to be a leader, he called himself the Son of God, and his followers were humble peasants!

Hung left his farm home. He gathered about him young, discontented men like himself until he had a great army. Then he proceeded to take over China. So successful was he that the Empress with all her imperial soldiers could not have withstood the T'ai P'ing rebels, had it

This charming scene, a combination of old and new China, was photographed one Sunday morning in Peking. The place is the new King Chan park, new because it was constructed since the Liberation and for the pleasure of the people. Young people enjoy their holiday leisure on a park bench by the lake. They are probably students.

The old professor, however, has to work. Yet he, too, enjoys the fresh air of the park. Shaded by a paper umbrella, very old style, with the traditional palm leaf fan awaiting the noonday heat, he is correcting papers, the eternal student papers that burden the life of any professor anywhere. His desk is a handsome boulder—no garden or park in Asia is complete without rocks—and he uses a rock as a seat. It appears that he is resolutely old-fashioned, for though a strolling student wears blue jeans—or the equivalent—the old professor has his baggy, old-fashioned trousers rolled up and over them a long cotton old-fashioned gown.

Peking. The Imperial Palaces are closed and silent under the snow. No one has climbed the marble steps or walked in the courts. The palaces are ghosts of the past. All life has departed. Only the beauty of the past remains. That beauty is eternal. The majestic sweep of the rooflines, the carved marble balustrades, the dreams, the designs, the creation of the builders and the artists of the past— all these remain.

not been for an English officer whom she employed to organize and lead an army himself. He is known in history as Chinese Gordon. Even so, the Empress might not have conquered had not Hung, overwhelmed by his own success—the Little Brother of Jesus, as he called himself—yielded to the temptations of power. He became corrupted by luxury in his capital at Nanking, the very city where I lived three quarters of a century later, and he fell from his high position and lost his holy war—lost it, but not without having lost with him over twenty million of his compatriots.

The story of this mighty rebellion I heard first from Wang Amah and therefore from the point of view of a humble person. She had been a young girl at the time and so pretty that her family, who lived in Yang-chow, across the river from Chinkiang, where we lived, had kept her at the bottom of a dry well to preserve her from the rapacity of the rebels. Later, of course, I studied the story in detail from historical sources as I prepared to write my long novel about the Empress Tzu Hsi, entitled *Imperial Woman.*

As for Wang Amah, she lived to see me ready for college and although she had retired, she came back to pack my clothes, for she trusted no one to see that every button was on and all was pressed and neat. She died during my freshman year when I was far away in the strange country of my ancestors, the United States, and I shed my sorrowful tears alone. God rest her dear soul!

Mr. Kung, or Teacher Kung, as I properly called him, introduced me to quite a different Chinese group. Wang Amah represented the humble folk who kept small shops in cities and towns. I suppose that none of her family could read or write. Mr. Kung, however, came from the intellectual elite, a scholar of the old school, a gentleman of courtly, formal manners, who had been recommended to my scholarly father by Chinese friends as a suitable teacher for a small, strongly individualistic American girl with a restless, inquisitive mind.

For ten years this dignified Chinese gentleman came to our house and instructed me in reading and writing Chinese, and in Confucian philosophy and manners. He taught me Chinese brush character-writing in the Confucian style. I began as a small child and as all small Chinese children do when—and if—they go to school. A piece of thin, transparent paper was put over a page of large, printed characters, very black, and I brushed over each as exactly as possible. It was a complicated process. First my brush pen must be held in the correct position, the bamboo handle, pencil-sized, between thumb, forefinger and middle finger of my right hand. The hairs at the end of the handle were rabbit hairs, about half an inch long, very fine and soft. This brush must be brought to a point on the ink block, where ink had been previously prepared by a few drops of water over which was rubbed the stick of dried ink made of lampblack, soot, or some other substance. Nor was this all. Very important indeed was to learn the order in which the strokes must be brushed. Each stroke had its own name, which at first Mr. Kung called out to me in a loud, clear voice. When I had perfected the sheet of tracing through the thin paper, I was then allowed to write the characters without trace paper.

Read aloud, each character had its own name, tone, and aspirate. The Peking Mandarin has four tones, but each consonant is either aspirated or unaspirated. Thus *p*, for example, is either aspirate—that is, sharply sounded with the breath—or dull without breath. Sharp *b* resembled, but not exactly, dull *p*. The Chinese ear is extremely sensitive to such differences. Mr. Kung corrected my Chinese speech to the extent of eliminating certain earthy phrases which I had picked up from servants, tradesmen, farmers and their children, chair bearers, and so forth. I was a fearless child, an inveterate roamer, and Mr. Kung was fastidious. Fortunately we lived in the Mandarin-speaking area of Kiangsu Province. Mr. Kung spoke the pure Peking Mandarin of the aristocratic literati. He corrected my colloquialisms and eliminated the sharp, uplifted fifth tone which had crept into our region because we lived at the important trade junction of the great Yangtse River flowing west to east across China and the Grand Canal, connecting south to north. Peking Mandarin has only four tones and its syllables flow in a majestic rhythm suitable to imperial life, whereas Cantonese, with its nine tones and crackling consonants, is suitable for tradesmen.

In short, Mr. Kung's duty was to add polish and grace to my already

In beautiful and ancient Peking an old-fashioned Chinese calligrapher sits at his Chinese desk. Upon it are his brush holder, his ink stone and slab, paper and paperweight. A calligrapher in China ranks as an artist. His writing of Chinese characters must show strength, grace, and above all, individuality. Note the way this one holds his brush, and note, too, the position of his left hand. He is totally absorbed in producing a work of art. I see by his brushwork that he is an excellent calligrapher. There is decision, there is power, in his strokes.

Even more interesting to me, however, is the painting of horses on the scroll hanging on the wall behind the calligrapher. The characters are too faint in the shadow for me to be able to decipher the name of the artist. The horses are so magnificent that I wonder if the artist can be the great one, Ju Peon? He painted horses as no other artist ever has. Alas, once I almost owned a scroll like this! He wrote me from China, years ago now, that he was sending me a painting of horses he had just finished as a gift for me. Not daring to send it by mail, he was entrusting it to a mutual friend to deliver to me, a Chinese writer then lecturing in Chinese universities but returning soon to his home in New York. I waited eagerly. The friend arrived. There was no mention of the painting. Later it appeared on the wall of his own study. Alas again, my inbred Chinese courtesy, drilled into me by my old Confucian teacher for ten years of my childhood, forbade my mentioning my loss to either friend, writer or artist.

native Chinese language and behavior. He had his moments of anguish and once even made efforts to resign since, after all, I was only a girl. A raise in salary and pleas from my parents prevented his resignation, to which were added my own efforts and promises, for I truly revered the elderly, dignified gentleman. I knew him to be good and I trusted him.

Since those years I have had added reason to be grateful to him, for through him I came to understand and appreciate the upper classes, the true gentry, the traditional elite of old China. I have never been more grateful than I am today, for it is possible that we shall never again have such people in China—or even in the world. The great revolutions of our age have upset society everywhere. Those who were high have been brought low, and those who were low are now in power. In China today, so I am told, the learned elite, if any remain, are required to spend a certain amount of time in manual labor, this in order to unite the people in a common life. To me, trained in another age, this seems an incredible loss of creative, intellectual energy. Only the future can tell whether I am right or wrong.

At any rate, Mr. Kung led me gently but firmly into his world. I was familiar with it through my parents' friends, but I had not been in it through my own experience. Now I became a part of it. As I grew in body and mind, I ceased to spend so much of my time with neighbors and chance acquaintances. My taste was formed under Mr. Kung's gentle, aristocratic hand. True, my parents were themselves aristocrats and intellectuals, but they were Americans and therefore foreigners, and their information and directions were not pertinent to my life in China, than which I knew no other. From Mr. Kung, therefore, I learned to find my intimate friendships among the young intellectuals, then moving toward their own revolution. But more of them later.

For before I pass on toward my own maturity, I must give full due to those who in a measure, under Mr. Kung's influence, I outgrew. I have spoken of Wang Amah. Shall I not also speak of our gardener, Lao Liu, who helped me plant my own small garden, filching seeds and plants and manure until my mother wondered every summer why my tiny garden bloomed more brightly than all her borders? It was Lao

Liu who stood weeping in the doorway of my father's study, wiping his eyes on his blue cotton jacket, while my father gave me one of two spankings which were the only punishments I received in childhood—not because I was not frequently naughty, which I was, but because my parents were gentle and intelligent and knew that words were more effective than blows. The unforgivable sin, however, was to tell a lie, and when I was about five years old, I told two in rapid succession, doubtless as experiment. The first I do not recall, but the second was concerned with the breaking of a small hand rake—unimportant except that I said I had not broken it when I had. Lao Liu, hearing of what was going on in my father's study, flew to intercept, but my father continued in his duty, whereupon the tender-hearted Lao Liu insisted it was he who had broken the rake. My father finished what he had begun, nevertheless, while Lao Liu wept, and I ran away, sobbing, to the servants' quarters, to be comforted by them all as they gathered to hear, with shocked exclamations, that a father could "beat" his own child. I was given cakes, peanuts, and whatever was handy. I remembered, however, in spite of all this, never to tell lies again.

And shall I forget the farmers and their families who lived in the valleys encircling our hill? I played with the children and learned games that later I taught my own American children. I learned folk songs, and reveled in wandering jugglers, traveling with tricky little monkeys trained to beg for pennies in a basket or bumbling bears lumbering with outstretched paws.

We lived outside the city, for my mother wanted the pure air and space to which she had been accustomed in her ancestral home. Yet I loved the city, too. Thither we went to buy material, the lovely, inexpensive silks, thick and soft and durable, from which my mother made her dresses. The shops, the outdoor markets, so much richer and more colorful than our American supermarkets, the variety in vegetables, fruits, and produce so much more than ours—why do we not have pomelo, sweet and easy to peel, instead of only grapefruit, and why not the endless varieties of oranges—shall I ever forget the sweetness of the big honey oranges? But let me not begin on such differences. Chinese, rich or poor, are gourmets, and it was there I learned what makes fine food. I never knew or shall ever believe that China was poor. True, we lived in the rich delta region of the lower Yangtse, but later I lived in the north and traveled near and far, and save when there was the freak of a flood or drought, I saw no endemic poverty—nothing, in fact, to compare with the endemic poverty of India.

And shall I ever forget the magic of the Chinese streets at night? They were not sinister or dangerous. I could stroll along their cobbled length and enjoy the brightness not of streetlamps regularly spaced but of homes and shops, their fronts open until late when the boards were slipped into their places for the night. Customers came and went, children played in the light of the oil lamps shining from homes into the streets or from lanterns hung from the eaves; families gathered about a table for their evening meal and shouted their greetings at friends passing by and, the meal over, men and women, if it was summer, gathered outside to sit on bamboo stools or stone doorsteps to call to each other in cheerful neighborliness or engage in some brief quarrel, enlivening the neighborhood thereby. Indeed, my question, when I returned to America to live, was to wonder where the people were and why they shut themselves in houses. There was a certain gaiety about life in China, with occasional flashes of violence, to be sure, but everything was in the open, or so it seemed to me in those days when I felt no danger and when I understood what I heard and saw and to a measure shared in it all.

Thus when the days of revolution came, I was not ready for it, though I had been very young when the old Empress died in 1909 and left a child as her heir and an aging and weak man as Regent. I was too young except to know that anger and fear had been rising among the people. It is difficult to describe that miasmic atmosphere of change. I am sure that it announced the end of any and all dynastic change in China, at least for the time.

But this change was more portentous than mere dynastic. For three hundred years white men of the West had been encroaching upon Asia. Asia is old, very old, and the West is young, very young. There is a generation gap between nations as there is among people. Long ago

Asia had rejected aggressive war as a wasteful process. As a result of this rejection, Asian countries had purposely not developed the weapons necessary for aggressive warfare. With weapons, therefore, the West was able to encroach upon Asia, first with trade and religions and then with weapons and wars. In alarm, the old Empress had tried to check such encroachments but she failed, and as a result of her failure, especially in the Boxer Rebellion, the revolutionary group increased in strength. Curiously enough, this group was led by young Christians, the graduates of missionary schools and colleges. Sun Yat-sen, their leader, was himself a Christian. Of the overthrow of the Imperial Throne, I have written elsewhere. It came about when I was a young girl still living in my Chinese house, and it was followed by ten years of increasing restlessness throughout the nation—restless because Sun was unable to establish a government, but restless, too, because the young intellectuals were burgeoning in every direction. New writers, new artists, all young, all enthusiastic with hope, enriched my circle of friends.

When I write these words, the face and figure of that magnetic young poet Hsu Tse-mo appears in my memory. He came often to see me, and there in my Chinese living room—my own, for by this time I had finished college, was back in China, and married—we discussed everything that was going on, politically and intellectually. Dreams seemed realities, Communism was not yet a threat, and hope infused every thought. Hsu Tse-mo was tall and superbly handsome. Yet it is his hands that I remember. They were not small but they were perfectly shaped in beauty and of the color of ivory. Alas, all was lost too soon, for he was killed in an early plane crash, one of China's first.

Yet there were many others. Hu Shih and Ch'en Tu-siu were leading the literacy revolution, Hu Shih in particular insisting that the written language of China should be the same as the spoken. Heretofore, the written language was *wen-li*, archaic in form, very beautiful but very difficult, almost as if in written English one were compelled to use Latin. Hu Shih defiantly wrote his monumental—but too often unfinished—works in the vernacular. My own scholar father, always of independent mind, had preceded Hu Shih by translating the New Testa-

It is the old man, the white-bearded old man, who gives meaning to the picture. How wise, how beautiful. True, he no longer wears his usual long satin robes. Instead he wears new long pants, an ill-fitting jacket. This does not matter to him. He knows everything. He has lived through it all. He turns his back on past and present and goes his own way. Nothing lasts forever. He knows that.

ment of the Christians into the Chinese vernacular. As for Ch'en Tu-siu, he led the literacy revolution toward the left—too far, some said —but he died young, before he could fulfill his promise. As for Hu Shih, he left China when Communism came in, and indeed served for years as Ambassador from China to the United States. During those years, after I had left China, we met often, we helped each other in various causes for China, and then he, too, died. He was representative of a stage in Chinese modern history.

And shall I forget Lin Yutang, that sprightly, brilliant, intellectual whom I knew first when I met with other young intellectuals in his Shanghai home? He was writing his witty, acid articles then in *The China Critic,* and these I so enjoyed that I introduced him to my own publisher in New York, who became his publisher. When Communism came into power in China, Lin Yutang and his family came to the United States and so did I. And he and his family spent much time with my own new family in Pennsylvania. During those years he wrote his brilliant books, among which I think the finest are *Moment in Peking* and *The Importance of Living.*

Nor do I forget the circle of young actors in Shanghai and especially Mei Lan-fang, the great actor who was the most famous female impersonator perhaps of all time. I visited him in his beautiful Peking home and ate the delicious Tibetan, sweet, cream-filled pastries in which he delighted and could not resist, although with his enjoyment he suffered agonies of self-reproach in his efforts to keep his figure slim as a young woman's.

Those were scintillating and wonderful days. We were all full of hope and plans. Encouraged by the new freedoms, young newspapers and magazines appeared like flowers in spring. Young men and women loosened old bondages. The family remained as strong as ever, but even the elders realized the reasonableness of choosing whom one would like to marry and allowed sons and daughters at least to meet those to whom they had been betrothed perhaps since childhood. Bound feet disappeared except in the hinterlands of North China. And I, not yet ready to begin my own writing career, was meeting, as a professor in two Chinese universities, the young men and an increasing number of young women who were my pupils.

After the Second World War and the triumph of Communism, all the bright young people scattered and disappeared. A few joined the Communists, those who could escape came to the United States, but most of them sank into the vast unchanging mass of the Chinese people. For while governments changed and wars were fought, lost, and won, the solid Chinese people, those on the land, of whom I have written so much, those in little shops in village, town, and city continued as they have for centuries. Dynasties have come and gone, governments have risen and fallen, rulers lived and died or been murdered, and the people go on, yielding for a brief while to brief change, and then resuming their lives again in the eternal family pattern, the central pattern of China.

Has this pattern now been disturbed? Disturbed but not destroyed! Communism has attacked it, as it has been attacked before. Communism has tried to force parent from child and generation from generation; it has tried to break up the ancient clans and break apart the secret societies. For a while it seemed to be succeeding, but inexorably the old pattern is creeping back. Children are at home again and grandparents have returned from old people's homes. They are taking care of the children as they always have, while the parents, the strong, middle generation, go out to work. Yes, they work in communes, but slowly the old design is appearing. Even the land is coming back in small private plots, limited by the State, it is true, but allowed, and the markets have private produce in them. Even the Chinese Communists cannot destroy the basic patterns. They can only use them and to the extent that they do use them depends the success of the Communist government and the length of its life. Nothing and no one can destroy the Chinese people. They are relentless survivors. They are the oldest civilized people on earth. Their civilization passes through phases but its basic characteristics remain the same. They yield, they bend to the wind, but they never break. The basic elements never change. More people in the world speak the Chinese language than speak any other.

There are more Chinese than any other people in the world. They have remained an entity, unfragmented, longer than any other people in history. Changes are peripheral and temporary; they are tolerated but only until their force subsides. Then the eternal pattern appears again. Appears? It was there all the time! It will be there forever, whatever its temporary name and government.

II

It was there all the time. This is the key to China's past and it will be the key to China's future. Her history has developed out of Chinese human nature. "Under Heaven," they say, "all men are one family." Heaven is the father, Earth is the mother, human beings are the children. The children live under the authority and the mandate of the father—that is to say, under Heaven. For the Chinese, Heaven is not a place. Heaven is a personage, undefined, with neither shape or form. Heaven is Being. A peasant, scowling at an angry sky pouring rain upon his ripe rice, ready for harvest, will shake his fist at the sky and curse *"Lao T'ien-yeh,"* or Old Heaven. All events, both good and ill, are the will of Heaven. Heaven directs the fate of the humblest man who lives in a thatched hut, but also the fate of the imperial ruler in his palace. Therefore, the people trust their ruler until Heaven no longer protects him. For centuries the Emperor was the intermediary between the people and Heaven. At the set and proper times the Emperor ascended the great marble altar in Peking and addressed Heaven on behalf of the people and offered sacrifice for them. The people put their trust in the Emperor as their representative before Heaven. So long as times were good and the people prospered, the Emperor was said to have "the mandate of Heaven." If the Emperor became weak and corrupt, as inevitably happened when a dynasty continued too long and the imperial blood thinned, or if evil times fell upon the people as the result of wars, earthquakes, or catastrophes of one kind or another, the people no longer trusted their Emperor. Lacking this trust, they declared he had "lost the mandate of Heaven" and a new Emperor must appear.

When this moment arrives, the country goes into a sort of fragmentation. Government is local, under civil servants, and, in the past, family tradition continued firm in its control upon the individual. Who was then to become the new Emperor? Contenders arose. These are always young men, daring and ambitious, each of whom gathers about him an army of young men, and they fight in a series of local wars, until local wars spread into national competitions, very much as football teams do in the United States, until finally one young man emerges as the victor. The people in the past then declared he had received "the mandate of Heaven," they settled down contentedly to a new dynasty, and life went on as usual. Even Communism in China arrived in the old patterns. Indeed it could not have succeeded had it not done so. Mao Tse-tung knew this very well. When he emerged as the victor over the Nationalists, he immediately assumed the position, though not the name, of the Emperor. The people, realizing that he had the mandate of Heaven—that is, empirical if not imperial power—fell obediently into the ancient and traditional place as subjects in fact if not in name.

Now that Mao Tse-tung is nearing the end of his life, his power is weakening; the people are quietly anticipating a change; contenders are secretly planning and even preparing. No one perhaps speaks aloud the old phrase, but be sure it is there in every Chinese mind and memory. What change will come, who will be the new ruler, no one knows. But one dynasty is ending and inevitably the new dynasty approaches. Whether one likes the old phrase or not, it is "the mandate of Heaven," in spite of all mankind.

What shall we of the West do to prepare ourselves for the next new mandate of Heaven in China? We must now return to the history of the Chinese people before the age of Western colonialism in Asia. The Western influence was a disturbing interlude, but only an interlude, in Asia and especially in China. It disturbed but did not destroy the permanent and ancient culture of China, that culture which the Chinese themselves created, developed, and established and which in turn created and developed and established them into a permanent and unchanged national personality. The West has not changed the Chinese people. They have only been disturbed—and only briefly at that.

There have been many books written upon the history of China. Many of them are good, some are excellent. I do not propose to summarize any of them. In brief, let me simply say that the Chinese are the oldest congregate of people now living on earth, that they began as nomads and hunters roaming the wilds of Asia, that they were the discoverers of fire and thereafter of cooking. The story I was told as a child by my Chinese tutor was that a boy was left in the family hut to guard the fire while his father was hunting and that as he played with the fire, as children will and should not, the hut itself went afire and thereby roasted the family pig. The father returned to find the boy licking his fingers from eating roast pig, and delaying punishment, he too tasted roast pig and immediately forgave his son. But Chinese are disconcertingly the first in many areas—gunpowder; rocketry; the family system which gradually developed into the clan system upon which Chinese society is so firmly based that I doubt even Communism has been able to displace it permanently; a form of government which discovers the natural leader and obeys him implicitly so long as he is worthy of the people's trust; an independence so sturdy and indestructible that when a leader is no longer worthy of trust he is displaced and replaced with relentless calm; an industrial and social life based on land; and a conservatism so prudent and practical that it resists all efforts of unrealistic idealists. Mao Tse-tung has ruled within this tra-

This starkly beautiful landscape is near the San Men Hsia Dam, on the Yellow River. San Men Hsia itself is a town in the western part of Honan Province. It has become, since the liberation, an industrial town. The name of the town in translation is Three Gates Gorges, this in reference to the famous three gorges of the Yellow River nearby. In today's New China the gorges are being drawn together in a great hydroelectrical station. Incidentally, during the excavations for this work, very interesting archaeological objects of the Chou Dynasty were found, among them bronze mirrors, weapons, cauldrons. But the whole area is interesting historically, for here the mythical Emperor, Yu the Great, who is supposed to have founded the Hsia Dynasty about 2000 B.C., controlled the waters of the Yellow River by cutting three passages, those which are now being united again.

However this may be, the landscape here is of bold terrain, sharp hills and terraced mountains. The road winds angularly up a steep hill, topped by a beautiful old Buddhist temple, now "liberated" into a school. In the foreground are straw stacks, roofed with clay, and a farmer with his loaded beast. Note the cave in the near foreground. It is probably used for storage, or perhaps as a shelter. The new Chinese are almost fanatically building or adapting shelters in case of attack from the Soviet Union.

dition and, as a result, is second in power only to the great First Emperor Chin Shih Huang, who in the latter part of the third century B.C. united the seven states of feudal China then at war with each other.

This emperor's story is brilliantly told in the great historical novel by Wilson V. Z. Faung, entitled *Chin Shih Huang, The First Emperor of the Chin Dynasty,* and presently published in Taiwan. This extraordinary Emperor, by strategy rather than warfare, united the seven states and set up the structure of the China of today. This was in 221 B.C. He did not believe in the freedom of the people and therefore he took over all the land and then redistributed it in what he considered the best way to use it for the good of all. Let me repeat—he did not believe in uncontrolled freedom for the people. Neither does Mao Tse-tung. Since he was the Emperor, Chin Shih Huang then divided China into thirty-six provinces. Each province was again divided into districts and the affairs of province and district were administered by three officials appointed by him and responsible only to him. One official was in charge of civil affairs, one of military affairs, and the third was an intelligence officer who reported directly to the Emperor on everything, including his two colleagues. His duty also was to tell the Emperor what the people themselves thought, did, felt, and said.

The system of government thus designed and set up by the First Emperor, Chin Shih Huang, endured for two thousand years and still endures today. A government must be the creation of a people or it dies before it can function. Mao Tse-tung in his own way is carrying on the Chinese tradition. He has reorganized Chinese society, to be sure, but so did the First Emperor. Literacy determines status but only to the degree that it is useful. Like Mao Tse-tung, the First Emperor gave temporary precedence to soldiers who were loyal to him rather than to their clans, for he needed their services in maintaining his empire. Second, were—and are—those persons who produced food. Third were artisans and craftsmen. The First Emperor was a great builder, and he delighted in the decorative arts. Under Mao Tse-tung, too, great bridges have been built and new buildings. There has been a revolutionary renaissance in the arts. Fourth were the useful literates, teachers, officials, and so on. Literates under Chin Shih Huang who were idle were considered useless—compare Mao Tse-tung here! And merchants came last. I do not know why, except that merchandise was and is, state-controlled.

Of course the First Emperor ruled by force, just as Mao Tse-tung does and as every successful Chinese ruler has done and must do if he is to keep the nation and people orderly. The Chinese people are opinionated, irrepressible, imaginative, resourceful, brilliant, and uncontrollable without force. Their base is still the home, the clan, the village, and to these they have always returned and will return again. By force, for example, the First Emperor built the Great Wall. Instead of sending idle persons and rebels to prison he sent them to build the wall. There they lived, died, and in it they were buried. Mao Tse-tung, however, has executed such persons. That is, he turned them over to those whom they had oppressed. It is reported that in the first year and a half under Communism, 1,300,000 such persons were killed. I cannot vouch for this. I do know that the "volunteers" sent from China to fight in the Korean War were those who opposed the Communist government—young Buddhist monks, Christians, criminals, men loyal to secret societies, and so on.

It was the First Emperor, too, who burned the books. The intellectual elite were his critics and he silenced them—as they were silenced by Mao Tse-tung and are being silenced in fields and mines today, if I can believe what I am told. And yet Mao Tse-tung is himself a scholar, a poet, a superb calligrapher, his brush writing fluid, strong, and characteristic. And he has greatly simplified the Chinese written language, so I am told. Yet, the First Emperor, too, was the first to use the brush in writing and to use straight lines rather than the later more elaborate curves. Both rulers have been practical men, however, subduing art to usefulness rather than pursuing it for its own sake.

Another great figure in the history of China was the Emperor Wu Ti, the most famous of the Han Dynasty, an era which coincides more or less with the beginning of the Christian era. Now he would be called a socialist, for he nationalized all of China's national resources in order to protect the poor against the greedy rich. Transportation was nationalized, too, as were all financial operations. Food and goods belonged

Here is the San Men Hsia dam when it was in construction. There is some essential modern machinery, but much of the carrying is being done in the old-fashioned way of bamboo baskets on shoulder poles. See, too, the high mountains through which the Yellow River flows, and the deep canyons its rushing waters have carved. The sources of the Yellow River are in the far west on snow-covered heights, and because of its hitherto uncontrolled floods it has for centuries been called China's Curse. Today, with such dams as this, it may become China's Blessing, not only because land is permanently redeemed but because it will furnish a source of continuing and permanent electric power for millions of machines and factories. Today the chief energy is still from human bodies—but tomorrow?

Of course now, as in ancient times, the Yellow River has provided also material for the arts, in music, operas and plays. Mao Tse-tung's actress wife, Chiang Ching, has greatly influenced the performing arts, and today they are charged with the propaganda inevitable in any revolutionary period, anywhere in the world. Among the new operas of New China is *Huang Ho,* or *The Yellow River,* naturally a great favorite with its crashing music, its thundering noise, and simple theme.

to the state for equal use by all, and prices were controlled. An income tax was imposed and huge public works set up to take the slack of unemployment. There is nothing new under the sun, indeed! China has already done it. But at length the people "tired" again of so much control, as the Chinese people always tire of control, and with Wu Ti's old age corruption crept in, laws slackened, inefficiency prevailed, and after a rebellion the Chinese went back to their old comfortable ways.

One might think such repetitions in history would discourage reformers, but no—a century later, Wang Mang as ruler set up a thoroughgoing socialistic experiment. This relentless character again gave land to landless peasants, controlled prices rigidly, started great public works with paid, not forced labor, took over mortgages from moneylenders and granted government loans, set up pensions for the old, the sick, and the jobless. Even school curricula were reformed—literary subjects were reduced and more practical subjects, such as geography, mathematics, history, and economics, were emphasized. Again under such control the people "grew tired." Taxes were heavy, corruption crept in and with it bureaucratic inefficiency. The people expressed their "tiredness" in increasingly alarming ways, such as revolutionary secret societies, until the old ways were resumed.

Yet a thousand years later an imperial chancellor, Wang An-shih, tried the boldest socialistic experiment of all until twentieth-century Communism took over Chinese government. Under Wang An-shih land and government loans were given to landless peasants, prices were controlled, trade and commerce were nationalized, welfare was provided for the unemployed, the old, and the sick, education was reformed, the classics were de-emphasized. Taxes of course were raised and, again, the people "grew tired" under strict control—so "tired" that the Emperor, to save himself, had to dismiss Wang An-shih and put an end to his "reforms."

Nevertheless, the idea of socialism has, in a vague way, continued to haunt the Chinese mind. Even in the Liang Dynasty, glorious as it was in culture and the creations of art, land was semi-nationalized in its use and control. And as late as the Ming Dynasty such attitudes prevailed toward the poor and the landless. Chinese socialism, however, is pervaded by the paternalistic concept of the ruler, the father-figure, responsible whether he be Emperor or Chairman.

Traditionally in China rebellion is most likely after the death of a strong ruler. The Chinese people grow tired of control. They want to "go home again," as they put it—that is, they want to return to the past. Certainly in my own youth I experienced the rebellion after a strong ruler. The Empress Tzu Hsi, the Old Buddha as she was called, became a legend before she died.

Hers is a dramatic story. She was born in Peking of a Manchu family. The family was poor, and she knew hardship and the necessity to work in the household. Nevertheless, as the Imperial law demanded, when she was seventeen, she was required, as were all young Manchu girls, to appear at the Emperor's palace and be prepared there for his inspection as a possible concubine. It was a doubtful honor, for it held the possibilities, even the probabilities of lifelong unhappiness. The Emperor was a weak man, his physical being damaged by the dissipating influences of the court eunuchs, and his mind and will undermined by a strong and conniving mother. In the palace reserved for concubines, there were those who had not been summoned to the Emperor's bed, or if summoned, perhaps only once, twice, or a few times, then forgotten. All the remaining years of their lives they spent in loneliness, their only companions women like themselves. Seldom did they give birth to sons, or even daughters for, it was whispered, the Emperor was impotent—if not altogether—then for long periods of time.

The real tragedy in Tzu Hsi's case, or Orchid, as she was called in her childhood home, was that she was already betrothed to a young man, Gung Lu, who belonged to her class. She loved him, and was deeply torn between love and ambition, for she had the power, she believed, to attract the attention of the Emperor, if she so willed. It was true that she was handsome, her golden skin smooth and fine, her eyes large and very dark, her brows clearly though delicately marked. Beyond these gifts, however, she had a powerful and magnetic personality, which she could use to powerful effect. If indeed she became an imperial concubine, she could rise as high as she wished and wield whatever power could best serve her ambition.

Yet she loved Gung Lu. He was tall and striking in appearance, a young man of keen intelligence and strong, calm will. Already he was a minor official in the imperial palace, and if she were successful, she could raise him to any position she liked. At least she could keep him near her and depend upon his counsel and loyalty. The decision was difficult for her, but ambition won. She took from Gung Lu's own hand the imperial summons, for it was part of his court duty to distribute such a document to all Manchu maidens who came of age that year.

Thus Tzu Hsi began her imperial years. She went to the palace and was prepared for inspection, one of many others. Yet she was not like the others. She did not join in their excited chatter. Calm and proud, maintaining her usual silence, she allowed herself to be washed and dressed in new garments and on the appointed day, at the appointed hour, she went before the Emperor. His mother sat beside him on a lesser throne and shared in the inspection. One by one, they passed. The Empress Mother chose a gentle, mild-faced girl, among others. The Emperor chose Orchid. Purposely she had placed herself last, and apart from the others. What he saw was a proud young beauty. What his mother saw was a willful girl who would be difficult to control. What Orchid saw was a weak, pallid young man, weighed down by his heavy, gold-embroidered robes, who nevertheless argued with fretful stubbornness against his mother. In the end both girls were chosen. In the days to come, when the Empress Mother was dead, the two were to be known as the Eastern Empress and the Western Empress.

Significantly, Tzu Hsi was the latter. Therefore, all her reigning years she was to be compelled to deal with an ever-encroaching West. England had already seized India. Holland was fastening her hold on rich Indonesia. France was to take Indo-China. Against such encroachments Tzu Hsi set all her efforts. She became the Emperor's favorite concubine, and from him and from every corner in the Forbidden City, the imperial home, she learned to understand the political problems of China. Resolutely she set herself against the enemy West, struggling to keep China whole and entire, the strongest nation on earth, the oldest and the most proud.

The Imperial Mother died and now it was she who prevailed in the palace. It was she who attended and sat behind the curtain which shielded her in the Great Hall when the Emperor gave audiences and received reports from his officials over the entire nation. It was she who in the privacy of the night, advised him, coaxed him, cajoled him by every means she could devise to act with strength and power against the young, encroaching Western nations. In all this Gung Lu was never forgotten. He advised her, told her what to say to the Emperor, how to persuade him to action. And she, in turn, raised Gung Lu as high as she dared.

She bore one son. He was her only child. So strong a child he was, so totally unlike the Emperor, who grew more feeble every year until his early death, that mouth-to-ear gossip over the nation said that Gung Lu was the father of the Imperial Prince. With the death of the Emperor, nevertheless, the boy became the Emperor, and Tzu Hsi the Empress Mother, guiding his every action, instructing him. Alas, the young Emperor was as willful as his mother, and with the help of deceitful eunuchs, he slipped out of the palace at night, disguised as a commoner and yet secretly known everywhere, and gave himself up to dissipation. As a result, he died at the early age of eighteen. His mother mourned with all her heart, but she took over the government of the country with firm control. The Eastern Empress was at her side, a pallid, silent figure, whom she treated kindly but with negligence.

The rest of her long life Tzu Hsi devoted to holding back the Western powers. There were other problems, too. The Chinese were restless under the foreign Manchu rule and rebellions broke out here and there almost continually. The most serious was the T'ai P'ing Rebellion, led by the son of a peasant, surnamed Hung. This man, claiming to be a Christian and the Little Brother of Jesus Christ, gained an immense following among peasants and Tzu Hsi had more than she could do to vanquish his forces with her own, greatly enlarged for the purpose. It is entirely probable that she would have failed had she not engaged an

The Imperial Summer Palace surrounds a great pool. No, the water is not stagnant. I have been there and in summer. The lotus was budding and there were many goldfish. Some of the fish were old, and so huge that I wondered if they had forgotten they were goldfish. Water flowed in and out.

The palaces were empty when I was there, for the old Empress, Tzu Hsi, was already dead and the country was in the usual contention for a new dynasty and a new Emperor.

I stood by the red-lacquered balustrades and looked in the pool. It was a sunny day in June and the fish were shining as they darted here and there in the water. Across the pool I saw an elm tree was beginning to die.

I see now that it is dead.

English mercenary, Chinese Gordon as he was called, who trained an army and subdued the rebels. Even he might not have won had not the Little Brother of Christ and his followers yielded to the pleasures of power and become dissipated in their capital, the city of Nanking. As it was, the rebellion was bloody indeed, the loss of life mounting to some twenty million Chinese.

Thereafter the Empress ruled in solitary and ever-increasing power, except that the Western nations continued to encroach upon China until in final desperation, against the aging Gung Lu's advice, she yielded in 1900 to the folly of the Boxer Rebellion. But there my own memory functions very well for I was a child of eight, and my intrepid father stayed at his work while he sent my mother, my baby sister, and me to Shanghai for refuge, while he went on as usual. We were fortunate, however, for in our rich, central province, Kiangsu, we had an intelligent viceroy, wise enough and modern enough to know that swift reprisals would follow the Empress's edict that all white Western people in China were to be killed. Our Viceroy inserted a negative into her command, a bold, brave deed, and so our lives were saved.

The long story of Tzu Hsi's life went on. Reprisals did come, indeed, heavily, and she paid dearly and with her the Chinese people. But it was the beginning of the end for her and for the dynasty. She fled Peking with her entourage, but when defeat was clear, and not to be escaped or prevented, at Gung Lu's advice she returned, calm and proud, her spirit undefeated, and with her usual grace and, as though there had never been war or defeat, she won the hearts of her enemies, who could not believe her any other than she seemed, and indeed was, a great, imperial figure in the world.

A few years of calm old age, living quietly among the birds and flowers she loved, and in 1909 she died, leaving the people and the country to a baby emperor, a relative, Henry Pu Yi, who reigned for only four years. Later he became the puppet emperor for the Japanese conquerors in Manchuria in 1934, but after the war he renounced his actions, and he still lives in China today. And soon after Tzu Hsi's death, as soon as 1911, the revolution broke, again under the leadership of a peasant's son, Sun Yat-sen, and he and his followers ended all dynastic rule and opened the doors, ten years later, to the people of the north, the people of Russia, who by then had destroyed their own imperial and ancient government and were Communists.

This Empress, the last ruler of the Manchu, or Tsing, Dynasty, under which I spent the first years of my life, was always a figure of importance to me. True, she was already old when I was born, and the dynasty was nearing its end. When the Empress died, I was a girl of seventeen—very young, true, but not too young to catch the mood of alarm and impending change over the whole country. She had ruled so long and so absolutely that, in spite of her faults, chief of which, of course, was that she was a woman, the common people revered her and felt safe as long as she lived and called her Old Buddha.

The Manchu, or Tsing, Dynasty, which ended with her, had been a troubled one. Beginning about 1644, it was in fact a foreign invasion of Manchus, who took advantage of the problems which brought about the fall of the Ming Dynasty. That dynasty had restored the imperial throne to a Chinese ruler, for preceding it had been the first foreign invasion which set up the Yuan, or Mongol, Dynasty. The Mongols were strong and, I was told by my Chinese tutor, a rough, uncultivated people, who learned how to rule under the always highly educated and experienced Chinese Civil Service. The Chinese, conscious always of the superiority of their culture, seem never to have made a total military resistance to foreign invaders. There was no national army in the Western sense. Under Confucianism soldiers were considered to be the lowest class of society and a soldier son was a disgrace to any good family. Wars of aggression were rejected, and explosive weapons were considered inhumane and evil. Gunpowder, for example, after its first invention for war, was forbidden to be used as a weapon. Instead it was for pleasure only, in fireworks. The principles of rocketry, too, also first discovered by the Chinese, were not to be developed for warlike purposes, since they might injure persons who had nothing to do with a war. The Chinese realized that there would always be some discordant characters who enjoyed fighting. Let them, therefore, fight and even kill one another, and not persons who had no liking for or concern with wars.

An ancient stone horse, much larger than life size, was made by a sculptor of the Ming Dynasty, who created his dreams in heroic dimension. It is the duty of this horse, and other huge beasts, to guard the road that leads to the tomb of the Emperor Tchengtsou. This Emperor was one of fourteen Ming emperors buried in this area. Other Ming emperors were buried in Nanking, the Southern Capital, from whence the last Emperor fled at the end of the dynasty to take refuge in Formosa from the invading Manchus.

The interesting facts of this picture are, first, the farmer who rides a mule on an ancestral saddle probably as old as the stone horse, and yet horse, mule and farmer are near the great, new, modern Ming Tomb Dam and Reservoir, an immense engineering work, the dam itself being 627 meters long. The farmer, mule and, in fact, the horse, are not surprised by anything. But that is Chinese human nature. I recall that in one region in Central China, the first train and, later, the first airplane were boarded without surprise and with complete aplomb by Chinese farmers with baskets of chickens and other produce. The Chinese are easily amused but never astonished.

This humane philosophy had served the Chinese people well until less civilized nations attacked and invaded them, as the Mongols did, and later the younger nations of the West. Under the Mongols for the first time China as a whole came under foreign rule. The capital was established at Peking, and certain areas, known now as provinces in the north and as Yunnan, or Tibet, an independent country under authority to China, enlarged the Chinese area. The road through central Asia was opened again to Chinese and the towns prospered.

The Yuan Dynasty was interesting in its cosmopolitanism. People came from the Moslem East, and even from European countries, like the agelessly famous Marco Polo. Catholic missionaries arrived, and with them trade with the West in ideas and goods and technical skills. Chinese products went westward too—as, for example, printing and gunpowder, and beautiful art objects. In this Mongol Dynasty, the arts of the theater flourished, encouraged by these cruder rulers from the north to whom refined theater was a diversion.

The countryside suffered, however, for the new rulers confiscated large areas, and as usual it was the peasants who rose up and changed the situation. The Yuan Dynasty, indeed, was brought to its end in 1368 by a peasant group, called the Red Turbans, or as my tutor called them, *"Hung Maotse"*—a term signifying revolt and fierce anger.

A Chinese peasant from the eastern province of Anhwei, Chu Yuan-chang, took advantage of the Red Turban revolt and drove the Mongols beyond the Great Wall and established, in 1365, the Ming Dynasty—the word *ming*, meaning "bright." Under his reign and that of his son the Great Wall was repaired and various benefits carried out. Great trade expeditions were sent as far as East Africa, seven of them led by a hardy eunuch.

During the first Ming Emperor's rule, the capital was moved from Peking, which means Northern Capital, to Nanking, which means Southern Capital. Centuries later, Nanking became my home for seventeen pleasant years. Nanking is a unique city, surrounded by a magnificent wall, which includes so vast a territory that there is land enough to support the population in case of siege. There I lived in a pleasant house with a garden and a bamboo grove, the whole encircled, as all such houses were, by a high wall, through which we came and went by an iron gate. One of our relaxations was to take a carriage ride beyond the city gates and to visit the ancient Ming Tombs. The city wall had nine gates, the reason being, or so I was told, that when an emperor died, nine corteges, each resembling the others, made exit through the gates, so that no one knew which cortege really belonged to the dead emperor. At any rate, the approach to the tombs was an avenue of huge stone figures, soldiers and sacred animals.

The Ming Dynasty, though brilliant, was relatively brief, ending in 1644, when the Manchus took advantage of local troubles to invade China. The capital, after the first reign, had been returned to Peking. In spite of various progressive achievements, the luxury of the large estates brought discontent to peasants, and this, as always, brought revolt and national weakness. There were uprisings among the people, discontents and strikes, and popular anger against the eunuchs who assumed too much power at the Imperial Court—these within the nation while outside were attacks from Japanese pirates. One emperor, in the north, committed suicide, and in 1644 the Manchus took power. A southern portion under another emperor resisted for a while, but he yielded at last and escaped to Formosa, or as it is now called, Taiwan.

In the days when I lived in Nanking, the revolt came again, but after the end of the Ts'ing Dynasty. In 1911 the entire government of China was overthrown by young men trained, for the most part, in Western missionary schools. After a period of unsuccessful struggle, harried by contending warlords, they accepted the offer of the Communists of Soviet Russia to help them. Against these, in turn, Chiang Kai-shek rebelled and set up his Nationalist government in Nanking. Then I lived under his rule, until it became obvious that Japan would attack China.

Chiang Kai-shek had set himself with all determination to learn how to form a republic and how to make a modern nation from a very ancient country. He was handicapped first by lack of experience. He was a soldier above all else. Therefore he had to educate himself in entirely new ways. Even his knowledge of the modern world was limited. He had never visited the West. A few years of military education

General Ma was the Governor of Shanghai before the Communists took over. He looks the well-fed plutocrat.

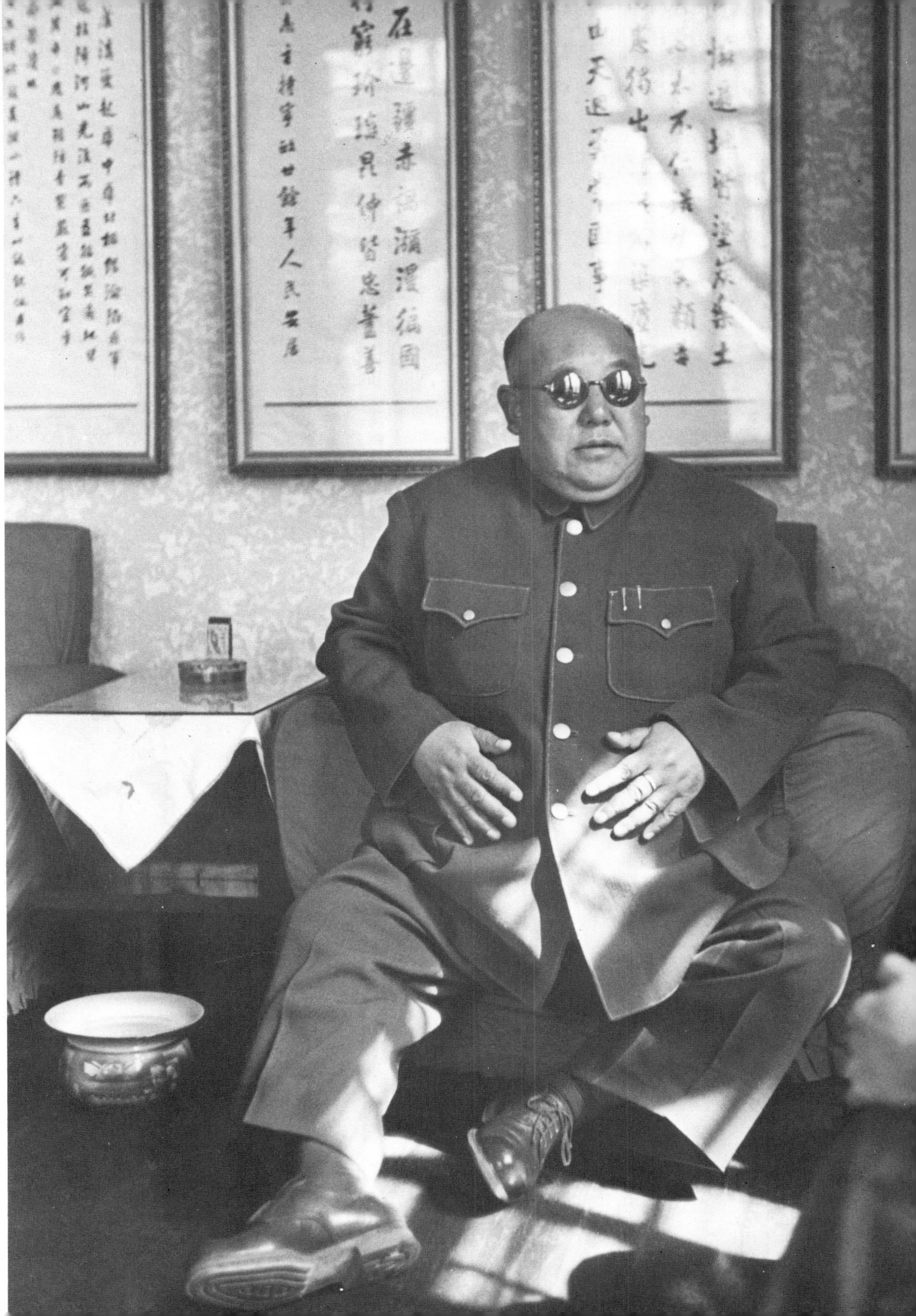

A picture of the temporary friendship between the army of the Republic of Nationalist China, led by Chiang Kai-shek, and the army of the Chinese Communists, led by Mao Tse-tung. They united in 1937 to fight the Japanese, and shared a mountain stronghold, where this photograph was taken. On the left is the flag of the Communists, on the right the flag of the Nationalists. You can see the Communist star on the caps of the two soldiers on the right. The other soldier is a Nationalist. The friendship didn't last long.

This is a lovely scene. Mountains soar in the distance. A large fish pond is in the center. Steps lead to a narrow dock, and trees shade the opposite bank. In the foreground are fields of vegetables, protected from frost or sun—I do not know which. A peasant carries two baskets on a shoulder pole. A handsome building is in the distance to the right—a temple? An ancestral hall? Perhaps just a large comfortable country home—we do not know. Nevertheless, a road, winding through the well-kept countryside, does lead to a large, comfortable country home. The buildings surround a central court—perhaps even a threshing floor. A wooded hill rises behind it.

In any country this would be a well-to-do home. It is the house where Mao Tse-tung was born and grew up. It is his ancestral home in Shaoshan, Hunan Province, China. From here he went to school and later to a university. Did he ever work in the fields? Did his father and grandfather work in the fields? I cannot answer my own questions. No one seems to know. But it is a lovely place in which to be born and grow up. Fortunate Mao Tse-tung!

in Japan, some months in Russia—these were the limits of his experience beyond China.

Nor did he dare to disband his army. China was divided by warlords, contenders for a nonexistent imperial throne. They were a historical and normal group, and in times past the victor became the new emperor who founded a new dynasty. Now, in spite of there no longer being any throne, they still contended in small wars. So long as they existed, Chiang Kai-shek could not disband his army, formed by those who had followed him when he left the Communists. With this personal army he fought one contender after another, killing some and bargaining with others, in his effort to unify the country under his single control.

All this went on while Chiang Kai-shek also pursued the Communists and drove them mile by mile through the incredible Long March into the far northwest of China. It is doubtful that they could have maintained their solidarity in the face of such hardships as they endured had it not been for the appearance and leadership of Mao Tse-tung. This man, the son of a well-to-do peasant, was himself a convert to Communism who had been ejected because of his differences with orthodox Communists. Most important of these differences was his conviction that the peasants must be recognized as a necessary force in the revolution. There had never been a successful revolution in Chinese history except when peasants and intellectuals joined together. Under his persuasion and leadership the Chinese revolutionary emphasis was placed upon the peasant and has so continued. Whether the course of nature will again sort out human beings according to their natural individual abilities, the future will tell. Intelligent and resourceful persons in any people inevitably rise to the top. There they again form an elite, against whom the ineligible will inevitably rebel, and so runs the ceaseless rise and fall of nations. And nowhere is this more true than in China, where intellectuals rose out of peasant groups, if those individuals could distinguish themselves by passing the Imperial Examinations, from whence they could pass to administrative posts in government, or, if they failed, at least become teachers, therefore intellectuals, therefore elite.

As President of the Republic of Nationalist China, Chiang Kai-shek struggled heroically with the problems of a disturbed era, chief among which was the setting up of a viable government. It was a time of uncertainty. Much has been said and written of corruption and huge sums laid away in foreign banks. Without condoning such practices, it must be remembered in all fairness that it was quite possible that Chiang Kai-shek and his government officials might fail. In this case there would be no place to which they could escape. Their only security lay in funds which they put away abroad. In any country in such circumstances the hoarding of private funds is probable.

Nevertheless the Nationalist government made definite achievements. Provincial colleges and local schools were opened, roads were built, and a form of government seemed to be evolving. Given time and peace, the Nationalist government might have succeeded. Chiang Kai-shek might even have been a good First Emperor of a new dynasty. Certainly his new and Western-educated wife, Soong Mei-ling, would have made a handsome and helpful Empress.

Alas, there was neither peace nor time. Chiang Kai-shek separated himself from the Communists in the spring of 1927. In 1931, long before he could establish an effective government or even unite his country under one rule, the Japanese took Manchuria. He turned to the West for help, even for a statement of disapproval. Silence was the answer. There were trade reasons why England kept silent. The United States uttered a mild protest through a single official voice. Meanwhile Japan continued her way south, basing her plans on the territory she had been given, in China, by the Western powers, at the end of World War I.

It was all too much. The Chinese Communists came forward to assume leadership in the universal anger of the Chinese people. This anger was centuries old. Again and yet again Japan had directed the land-hungry ambitions of an island people toward the vast areas of China. She had last attacked in 1894 and had at that time kept the island of Formosa, among other footholds, while Russia, as mediator at China's desperate request, had demanded the Maritime Provinces.

Yielding to the forcible demands of the Communists, who had "kidnapped" him, Chiang Kai-shek expediently combined with the Chinese

This is a picture of Mao Tse-tung and important members of his family. It was taken in Mao's birthplace in Shaoshan, Hunan Province, China. His was not a poor family, as one can see. On the left is Mao Tse-min, Mao's younger brother. Then come Mao's father, his grandfather, and Mao Tse-tung himself. The younger brother obviously wears a school uniform. The others wear the traditional long Chinese gown. Father and grandfather wear formal jackets of black satin over their satin or silk robes. They also wear the traditional small black skull caps with red buttons of knotted silk. The grandfather sits in the seat of honor at the right of the decorated table. The father sits in the next seat of honor. Mao Tse-tung, as eldest son, stands by the grandfather. His younger brother stands properly by the father.

I am interested in Mao Tse-tung's young face. It is rebellious, unsmiling, stubborn. It is like the faces of many young men in the world today.

This is another photograph of Mao Tse-tung. It is an old one, taken in 1934, on the famous Long March. Mao, sitting astride his little white horse, is directing his 100,000 people to what he firmly believes is freedom.

His face is different now. True, the men with him are walking and Mao is riding. Yet, after all, he is the leader. He has a great work to do. He wears rough clothes. The countryside is barren and gray. He has far to go. He is responsible for many.

How different is this face from the face of the rebellious boy in his comfortable village home! This face, handsome as it is, is bold, confident, courageous and—yes, honest. The eyes look straight ahead. The mouth is sensitive but composed. It is no longer pouting and sullen. One can trust this face. It belongs to a man of feeling but firmness. He is on his way but he is the leader and others will inevitably follow a leader.

Of the thousands of pictures of Mao Tse-tung I have seen, this is the one I like best. I hope it is the most true.

This is Mao Tse-tung's cave home in Yenan. The open door leads to his rooms. In the next cave house Chou En-lai made his home. Liu Shao-chi, former President of the People's Republic of China, also lived there.

Here we see the interior of Mao Tse-tung's cave home in Yenan. This served as his headquarters after the Long March. This picture, taken in 1964, reveals a beautifully fretted window, a well-made table probably of fine wood. On the table is apparatus for writing, tea drinking, and so on. The desk chair is of good, though simple, traditional design. A square stool, cushioned with a mat, and a wooden bench supply seats for callers. The floor is of brick.

The design of the fretwork of the huge window is especially interesting in its variety. All the designs are traditional. I doubt the window is paned with glass. It is more likely a specially made rice paper.

At any rate, the room is interesting for here Mao Tse-tung read, wrote, and made his plans for the development of the modern revolution in China, which revolution is still in process. Here he planned his attack on Chiang Kai-shek and announced his determination to resist Japan.

In this quiet place, with its dignity and grave beauty, he was free to shape the life of his countrymen, and so he did and continues to do.

Communists to unite against Japan. It is doubtful, however, that the Chinese could have won, in their state of national turmoil, had it not been for the folly of Pearl Harbor. This brought the United States into the war as an ally of China, and saved that country entire.

It may be said, in answer to the foolish question of how "we lost China," that we never "lost" China, unless we consider our own folly in deliberately cutting ourselves off from China when the revolutionists took over and established a Communist, or as they like to call it today, a Socialist government. The facts are simple. During World War II, the Chinese forces, Nationalist and Communist, combined with Americans and fought battles against the Japanese on Chinese soil. When victories were won, Nationalists and Americans withdrew their forces to fight the Japanese elsewhere. The Communists also withdrew—but they always left a cell behind. When Japan was finally forced to surrender and the war ended, they surrendered in China to these Communist cells, the only ones left to receive surrender. Thus the whole of China belonged to the Communists.

One could have foreseen this, and indeed I did, but my spoken forebodings fell on ears deafened by ignorance. The struggle then to persuade Nationalists and Communists to unite was hopeless from the first, and I only marveled that Americans did not see it—and further astounded that we could cut ourselves off from the largest and, to us, the most important country of the world, China. Meanwhile Chiang Kai-shek, understanding from the first the hopelessness of his situation, took refuge as the last of the Ming emperors had done, in the beautiful and flowery island of Formosa.

There he and his family and their followers have lived, dreaming their dreams as all must do. Years have passed. He is an old man, dignified, reserved, proud. As for the United States, his ally, the island has provided an essential military base in maintaining the policy of what we have called "the containment of Communism."

This morning a Chinese friend, just returned from China, closes his long, detailed letter with these words.

"The Chinese people are growing tired. They want to go home again."

III

Among the thousands of great names in Chinese History, past and present, the name of Confucius far overshadows all others. Mr. Kung early impressed this upon me. As a consequence, from earliest childhood Confucius has shaped my thinking, my conduct, my personality. Confucius is my frame of reference. When I studied Greek philosophy I realized the resemblance between the teachings of Plato and the great Chinese, but the latter still prevailed, to my mind, in the combination of a lofty morality and a practical realism.

My friend, Lin Yutang, has said that in contrast to the Western nations, China is a nation of feminine nature. He does not mean this in a sexual sense, but in the practical realism that women have developed the world over. For China, I am sure this trait is due to the influence of Confucius which has there prevailed over every other until the coming of modern Communism in 1921. It is understandable that these modern reformers should first of all attack Confucianism and endeavor to eliminate every vestige of his influence. For he was realistic and practical. He did not indulge in large, speculative ideas. He was of concrete mind, with a real dislike for abstraction. He was evocative without being imaginative. He himself insisted that he was not a creator but a collator and teacher of the past. He was essentially original, however, in his search for the inner meaning of life. He was not religious—indeed, he eschewed all religions and declared that he had no interest in gods or the hereafter; yet he was a moralist in his belief in order and in his conviction and teaching that there is a right way to do everything in life, even to lying in the right position in bed before sleep. Order, decency, self-control, consideration for others, the proper behavior in any relationship, a discipline that begins first with oneself—these were his concerns. For how, Confucius inquires, can one be worthy of control over others if he cannot control himself? Yet all that is done must be within nature, in accord with the winds and waters, within the balance between *yang* and *yin*. Nor are *yang* and *yin* antagonistic forces. On the contrary, they are cooperative and thus form together the perfect circle of life.

As a Confucian, therefore, Mr. Kung taught me that the superior person is calm and controlled. He never loses his temper or lays hand on anyone. He is correct in all human relationships, giving to each his due, yet possessed by none. True, like Saint Paul in the Christian faith, Confucius had a low opinion of women, this the result, I daresay, of having a bossy, overbearing wife. In theory, therefore, he taught the subjection and inferiority of women. Since I grew up also under the teaching of my father, who thought highly of Saint Paul, I accepted my own inferior position as a female without concern or hostility. It was well that I did, for this early Confucian-Christian training prepared me for my later career as a woman writer in my own country. When I overstepped myself as a woman to the extent of winning the Nobel Prize for Literature and even of being next to the youngest among the prize winners, my education in China had prepared me for the pained outcries of American males who were themselves writers and critics. Indeed I felt for them and was even somewhat apologetic. Thanks first to Confucius and secondly to Saint Paul, I have greatly enjoyed my life as a woman and have been, though inferior, callously indifferent to male outcries since, joyously, I do as I please. For, as Confucius complained, what can one expect of a woman?

In brief, since China had no state or national religion, Confucianism supplied a basic moral order and declared the right way of performing every action. One knew who was a superior person and who was not. It is no wonder, therefore, that the young revolutionists in China, who were the young literati, should turn against the conventionalities of Confucius. Ch'en Tu-hsiu, for example, though he had passed the Imperial Examinations with honors, openly repudiated and even insulted Confucius. He traveled abroad to Japan and Europe, and founded a revolutionary newspaper in 1915 entitled *La Jeunesse*, which every literate young Chinese rushed to read. On its pages he berated the traditional values of Confucianism.

"Better," he once said, "that all our ancient culture should disappear than that our race perish by its inability to live in the modern world."

Though I was then in college in Virginia, I followed closely what my Chinese friends were doing and saying. Yet I could not forget Mr. Kung and the exalted concepts he had given me of Confucian ethics. To this day I shrink when I hear cheap "Confucius say" jokes. We Americans are as ignorant of Confucius as the Chinese are of Jesus. Yet in strange ways there are similarities between these two, though Confucius lived five hundred years before Jesus. Confucius grew up not knowing his own father and so he called himself the Son of Man, a phrase later used by Jesus. Confucius, too, was a wanderer, seeking his followers anywhere and everywhere. He was poor and was held up to scorn by the proud and successful, but he was indomitable and unchanging in his convictions. Some of his sayings are strangely Christian. It was he who first spoke the golden rule that Jesus later used: "Do not do unto others," Confucius admonished his disciples, "that which you would not have them do unto you."

The young people of China today are not being educated in the wisdom of Confucius, however. When Lin Yutang returned to his country even before Communism came to power, he was shouted down when he lectured on Confucianism. Today it may be that Confucius is all

This is the Temple of Heaven. It is in Peking. I have been there many times to enjoy its noble beauty, magnificent in its simplicity. The proportions are perfect. The three-tiered roof is of clear blue tile, darker than blue sky, somewhat lighter than royal blue.

Here the Emperor, the Imperial Person between Earth and Heaven, between Man and Deity, made sacrifice for his people at the proper seasons of the year and in the name of his people asked the forgiveness and blessing of Heaven. The concept of Heaven was like that in all religions. However many and diverse the gods, the Supreme Being was Our Father in Heaven—Lao T'ien Yeh. The Supreme Ruler on Earth—namely, the Emperor of China— was the only human being high enough in rank to approach the Ruler in Heaven.

Today in the People's Republic of China there is neither Emperor nor Heavenly Father. There is only Chairman Mao Tse-tung. Therefore, let the people come and go. Let the children play on the marble approach to the Temple of Heaven, let them climb the marble steps to the temple. Let them play upon the sacred altar itself, where once even the Emperor was compelled to kneel!

but unknown in the country he spent his life to save centuries ago by creating order out of disorder and morality out of immorality. Nevertheless, the words he spoke are immortal words because they are truth, and truth will someday prevail. On that day Confucius will come back to his own.

Meanwhile it is a strange course of events that his teachings and even his words are enshrined here in my American heart and mind so that they are part of my very being. I pause at this instant to gaze out of the window which my desk faces here in my Vermont study, upon as American a scene as can be found. It is the day before Christmas. The tree downstairs is trimmed and gifts are accumulating beneath its dripping silver tinsel. Boughs of holly have been cut from my family home in Pennsylvania—it is traditional that we spend Christmas in snowy Vermont, for skiing is part of the holiday fun—and holly is everywhere. Downstairs someone is playing Christmas carols. And here I sit alone, writing of another world and yet my world, too, for I live in it constantly, my mind, heart, and conscience forever shaped by a wise man who lived five hundred years before Jesus.

Like Jesus, Confucius was not honored in his own life. He visited rulers, admonished them, besought them on behalf of the people, endeavored to show them by precept and example how to be worthy of their high place and so fulfill their responsibilities. He was not, as I have said, a creator. He had no new gospel to proclaim. His treasure was the wisdom of the past, the wisdom of wise men. He says in the *Analects,* "I have transmitted and do not create anew. I am faithful to the wise men of old and I love them."

It has been the complaint of the young Chinese that Confucian self-control is intolerable. Yet his own personality contradicts this complaint. He discovered a psychological truth which Western psychologists have only recently proclaimed. Act as though you were the person you want to be, and you will become that person, we are told nowadays. But this is the very heart of Confucian philosophy. He taught that external behavior and control mold our inner being and thus our personality. Rites and manners, he taught, were therefore important, for rites unite society into a unified whole and good manners—courtesy, gentleness, altruism—create the good human being.

Confucius practiced his own doctrines, as all wise men must, but like all great men, he was not appreciated during his lifetime. When he was near his end he wept and said to his disciples, "No intelligent ruler has arisen to take me as his teacher and yet already my time has come to die."

Nevertheless, Confucian ethics became the foundation of Chinese society, though repudiated again and again by impetuous young reformers and revolutions. Yet when the revolutions died down and order returned, the order was always based on Confucian teachings and philosophy. Indeed it is basic that the strong, vital, emotional Chinese people be held in restraint—not the restraint of tyrants, which they never long endure, but the self-restraint which produces the only atmosphere in which life can continue with dignity and grace. Only in such an atmosphere can persons develop into the superior persons who alone, Confucius taught, are worthy of the people's trust.

I must not, however, give the impression that Confucius was the only man to shape the Chinese world in which I grew up. It was a world in which through thousands of years action was followed by reaction. Confucius crystallized the past for the guidance of the present and the future. This was his action. Reaction came in the form of another great figure, without whose philosophy Chinese civilization might have remained static and declined into stagnation. This second force was Lao Tze. There is among scholars a cynical doubt, occasionally expressed, that Lao Tze ever existed as a living person. Whether he did or did not is relatively unimportant. The fact is that a reaction to Confucian ethics, so controlled, so intellectually planned, certainly took place in history and probably it began in the emotions and brain of a willful, independent, contrary-minded human being, to whom has been given the name of Lao Tze. His philosophy was called Taoism.

Mr. Kung instructed me carefully also in the doctrines of Tao—not with the same enthusiasm, I must confess, as he had taught me Confucianism. He acknowledged, however, that the willful Lao Tze, in his

The famous Buddhist Caves of Lungmen, in Central China. They belong to the eighth and ninth century and are evidence of the missionary period of Buddhism. Each of the major religions of mankind, and this of course includes Christianity, has an aggressive or missionary period. Buddhism is no exception. Originating in India, its missionaries went to China, Korea, and Japan, among other Asian countries. There is solid evidence that Chinese Buddhist missionaries even reached the continents of North and South America.

The young people of New China were at first encouraged to learn about and respect their own ancient civilization. This picture, taken in 1965, shows not the pious pilgrims of pre-Revolutionary times but the Young Pioneers of New China, each with a red scarf, coming here to admire what their forbears had done. Now, alas, since the activities of the Cultural Revolution, with its avowed purpose of doing away with "old ideas, old culture, old customs, old habits," I do not know what has happened even in the beautiful and unique Lungmen Caves. Destruction of the great and noble past destroys not only the present but the future of any nation, and is a loss, indeed, to all peoples.

emphasis upon emotion, nature, and the individual, provided a release from the stern rigidity of a crystallized Confucianism. He advocated, therefore, a combination of the two. He said:

"Let your manners be Confucian, let your emotions and thoughts be of Tao."

Thus did he close his dissertations on Taoism. In fact, Taoism was necessary to the growth of Chinese culture and thought, for it provided opportunity for the development of the arts, particularly in painting and music. True, Confucius gave music a high place in the development of moral character and he himself loved music, traveling long distances to collect songs and melodies of the past. But Taoism provided the emotional freedom to create new songs and melodies as expression of human personality.

I was encouraged, therefore, by Mr. Kung to learn how to play a Chinese zither, called *yang ch'ing*. My mother, herself a musician, took great interest in this stage of my Chinese education and bought, under Mr. Kung's direction, a beautiful zither, lacquered in black and gold. The strings were delicately fine and made of brass. Upon these strings I played with two very flexible bamboo hammers, mere slivers but with tiny rounded ends. The music these made was graceful, poignant, and sweetly piercing. The melodies, of course, were in the Chinese pentatonic scale, roughly following A, C, D, F, G in our Western scale. The effect was plaintive and somewhat monotonous. Mr. Kung himself was an expert on the *yang ch'ing*, and I learned to do well enough, too. What became of this zither in the upset of later wars and revolutions I do not know. And today Taoism has become fashionable with the young avant-garde of the West. Of this I can only say that it is not the same Taoism that Mr. Kung expounded to me. Through his expositions I learned in my own way to feel as freely and creatively as I wished, but to carry myself outwardly and in some respects as a Confucian—also inwardly, at least in my love of order. To me the first essential in the creation of beauty is order. However handsomely a room is furnished, for example, there is no beauty without order.

The preeminent change in China's past was the entrance of Buddhism from India and its success there during the decline of the great

Han Dynasty. The form that Buddhism took was the Mahayana, a comforting and inspiring form, compatible with the practical Chinese nature. This new religion brought with it a contradictory principle which expresses concretely the basic difference between the people of India and the people of China. The people of India are deeply religious, concerned always with the development of the individual soul through this earthly life to the life beyond. The people of China have never been so concerned. Their thought is concentrated upon this earthly life, its order and its happiness. Therefore, religion has never engaged their primary attention. Hsün-tse, a philosopher and skeptic, was even against Taoism and he expressed it thus:

> You vainly seek into the cause of things;
> Why not appropriate and enjoy what they produce
> Therefore I say—to neglect man and speculate
> about Nature
> Is to misunderstand the facts of the universe.

Chinese philosophic thought has always been the organization of human life and its relation to nature. Even Chinese law was based on harmony with human nature, this in contrast to our Western legal system, which is punitive rather than humanistic. Harmony was the keyword in Chinese civilization and the person who lived in harmony with his fellow human beings and with nature was the civilized man. It was a philosophy of wisdom, productive of peace and self-control. Taoism did inject a certain mysticism into man's relationship with nature, but this was far from a religion. The consequence was an inner peace in the Chinese heart, a belief in *being* rather than in *becoming*. There was no sense of sin or, indeed, of evil. An act of violence was a failure in harmony rather than an evil in itself. Morality was harmony between man and nature, a union that approached a religion but was without transcendentalism. The result was superb civilization, orderly, graceful, and above all, peaceful, individually, nationally, and internationally.

The period of China's highest development was in the Han Dynasty (202 B.C. to A.D. 220). Even when I lived in China near the middle of the twentieth century the greatest compliment one could pay a Chinese was to call him "a true son of Han." Indeed, the influence of the Han Dynasty persisted through the centuries until the end of the Ch'ing Dynasty in 1911. There were certain innovations with each incoming dynasty, of course, but nothing so important, so basic, as the arrival of Buddhism from India through the medium of Indian Buddhist missionaries. True, there were occasional invasions into China by northern peoples from Central Asia, Mongolia, and Manchuria, but China absorbed them by intermarriage. If and when sections of China split apart under these attacks, it was temporary, and her basic unity soon asserted itself again.

Into such a disturbed period, however, Buddhism made its inroads, just as after the end of the Ch'ing dynasty, Communism came to China —after a period of dynastic change, complicated by attack from Japan. There is another similarity. Buddhism had passed its peak in India and needed revival. By leaving a weary people and taking its transcendental message to a new people, especially to a people so strong and invigorating as the Chinese, Buddhism itself was revived and invigorated. The Chinese made a fresh approach to old Buddhist theology. In fact, Buddhism did not take root in China until it was infused with the Chinese spirit and until it fell into harmony with Chinese culture—that is, until it became Chinese or Mahayana Buddhism. Exactly the same must be said of Communism in the twentieth century.

IV

I have been writing about my Chinese people day after day here in my Vermont study and this morning I face an American landscape in bright winter sunlight. It occurs to me, therefore, that I have not written on the landscape upon which the Chinese live. What of the land itself of China?

First of all is its diversity. I grew up among gentle hills but on our horizon were mountains. The highest of those mountains was Wu T'ai Shan, or Five-Peak Mountain, because it had five peaks. It was also the home of bandits who robbed the rich and helped the poor. This group is traditional in Chinese history, especially in times of political transition such as I have described and in which I lived my Chinese life. I am not sure that bandits always did help the poor, but they were supposed to do so and consequently were regarded with a certain leniency by people in general. Indeed, one of the masterpieces of China, the long novel *Shui Hu Chuan,* deals entirely with a brotherhood of

The scene is of a people's commune near Chungking, the Chinese wartime capital during World War II. It was, in 1957, a farm cooperative. These cooperatives were the precursors of people's communes. The cooperative had five thousand people belonging to it. The cheerful woman hurrying along the hilly path was the chairman of the cooperative. She was then thirty years old, she was self-educated, was married and had four children. Chinese women, generally speaking, are good executives. They are accustomed to managing the business of large households where, in traditional fashion, several generations lived together in as much harmony as possible. Everyone had to be fed and clothed and household work apportioned to the proper individuals. The spending of money had to be carefully managed.

It is interesting to note the loudspeaker affixed to the leafless tree at the left. This was, and perhaps still is, used to pipe information and music to the workers in field and village.

The landscape is beautiful, for China is indeed a beautiful country. Misted mountains give way to rice fields flooded for the seedlings, even the hills are terraced. A homestead here and there adds stability and human interest.

robbers, one hundred and eight in number—this being a sacred number in Buddhist lore—who developed the military tactics of guerrilla warfare. I translated it into English under the title of *All Men Are Brothers*—the publisher's title, to which I reluctantly and mistakenly agreed since he insisted that Americans would not understand the Chinese title.

This novel is one of the three great novels of China. Of the other two, the one entitled *Three Kingdoms* was long ago very ably translated by an Englishman, S. Brewitt Taylor. The third, *Dream of the Red Chamber*, has never been fully translated. A shortened version, unfortunately inadequate, does not give the rich flavor of this long and fascinating story. It is a tragic story of corrupted love, the hero the young son in a family of great wealth. He is surrounded and spoiled and ruined by the constant attentions and affections, jealousies and ambitions, of bondmaids, concubines and female relatives in the huge family circle. Translation is further complicated by the many poems essential to the novel.

Shui Hu Chuan is entirely different from either of the other novels. It is a rough-and-ready story of rough-and-ready men, ruthless men, shaped by injustice and governed by a crude mixture of ruthless revenge and a desire to help others like themselves, the downtrodden and the poor, whom society rejects.

A curious incident lingers in my memory in connection with the publication of my translation of this novel. When its date was announced, I received an invitation to a dinner in my honor given by the Chinese students in a nearby, great university. I accepted of course, and upon my arrival on the evening of the dinner, I saw I was the only Westerner present. This instantly conveyed to my Chinese-trained mind that the dinner had a purpose beyond mere honor. Nothing was said, however; the evening progressed pleasantly, the conversation was general. Only at the end was the purpose disclosed. The head of the organization rose and made a courteous speech to me, which he ended by requesting that I stop the publication of my translation of *Shui Hu Chuan*.

Amazed, I inquired what the reason could be for this unexpected request. Was the translation perhaps not good?

The answer was that, to the contrary, the translation was too accurate, and nothing had been changed or deleted from the famous original.

"What then?" I inquired.

The answer, given in detail, was that it would have been better had I *not* translated so fully, so accurately and faithfully, for in so doing I had revealed certain characters and incidents very unfortunately, for they could give a very bad impression to Americans about the Chinese.

"For example—" I urged.

Wusung, for example, was the answer, who not only ate dog's meat but under the stress of hunger ate human flesh and thereby gave the impression that Chinese could be cannibals.

I assured them that there were Western persons also who, under starvation, were known to have eaten human flesh, but I have never been convinced that my young Chinese intellectual friends were reassured. Nevertheless, I did nothing to stay or stop the publication of the book, and it has continued on its way and has been translated into other languages in Europe and elsewhere.

This sensitivity of the Chinese toward criticism continues to this most modern day. But I am not fair in calling it Chinese. It is in every country at certain times. When Charles Dickens visited the United States a hundred and more years ago, the sensitivity of the then infantile United States to any criticism was the phenomenon he observed everywhere he traveled and which he ridiculed most severely with bitter mirth. Yet he found it in certain people and groups even in his own old country and he ridiculed it there, too.

As for *Shui Hu Chuan*, I undertook the long labor of its translation partly because of its great and lasting fame in Chinese letters—I cannot say "literature," since the Chinese had a moralistic attitude toward all novels in those old days and novels were not considered literature or at best only *yea shih*, or "wild literature"—but mainly because the book revealed so important an aspect of Chinese life, the rebel aspect, I might call it, for there have always been rebels in Chinese history. Indeed, the right to rebel has always been considered an "inalienable" right and there have been many rebellions, the most serious those among peasants which could and often did bring an end to the existing dynasty. Since

Here we are in North China, in a peasant home near Peking. Potatoes grow well in this somewhat sandy soil. A farm wife is grinding dried potatoes into potato meal, which later she will make into noodles, stuffed bread rolls, and other delectables.

Her little daughter is being taught to help. Her small strength amounts to nothing, but she is learning a lesson for coming womanhood. Grinding wheat or corn or potatoes on the ancient stone quern is traditional woman's work.

In the background is the farmhouse. It is simple but comfortable, a few rooms about a court, perhaps, the front rooms for storage, the inner rooms for living. A shed, open to air but under roof, houses a yellow cow, a pig, a few hens—if it is so allowed now in this area. The walls are of sun-dried mud brick. They last well in this dry northern climate, keeping out heat in summer and cold in winter. They are untrustworthy in floods but this is not flood country.

It is winter. The trees are leafless. Woman and child wear cotton padded clothing. The sun is bright, however, for the shadows are black in the clear Peking air. This is a good season.

This flock of ducks in a commune near Shanghai are on their way to market. In a few days they will become a variety of delectable duck dishes in gourmet restaurants or even in private homes of Chinese businessmen. Ducks bring good prices in all Chinese markets, and it is therefore presumable that only persons with money can eat them. Peking Duck is, of course, the most famous duck dish, and it is now served in almost any important city in the world where Chinese restaurants do business. One may in China also eat salted duck.

These two duck farmers are suitably clothed and seem themselves well fed. They drive the ducks skillfully, keeping them within bounds by means of two long poles, probably bamboo.

my entire life until then had been lived during such a period in China, it was natural that I should find *Shui Hu Chuan* of peculiar interest and even importance.

There was another reason. When the Communist revolution rose in China, I observed that the Communists were following the exact guerrilla tactics that the robbers of *Shui Hu Chuan* had used five centuries and more before, and so I began my work. I spent four years on this translation under the illusion that if and when my American people were engaged in an Asian war—which even then seemed inevitable to me—they would know how to deal with Chinese Communist guerrilla military strategy and tactics. Mao Tse-tung always carries a copy of *Shui Hu Chuan* with him, I am told, and certainly the warfare in Vietnam has been based on this book. Alas, I doubt that any American military man has read my translation of this great novel!

Beyond Wu T'ai Shan were the rich fields and grasslands of Central China where we lived. The Yangtse River, in comparison to which the Mississippi is a brook, is a vivid part of China's landscape. Its sources are in Himalayan snows and it divides China into two areas, one called "North of the River" and the other "South of the River." Both are vast areas, for China is a third again as large as the United States and its landscape is even more various, from the tropics of the south to the icy deserts and bare mountains of the north. Great cities, thousands of towns, millions of villages shelter the people. Chinese do not live in isolated farmhouses as Americans do. Farmers live in clan villages and go out daily to work on their land. The Chinese are gregarious and do not like being alone. They like to talk and laugh and gossip, a lively, cheerful people who joke and make puns and enjoy food. Are they difficult to understand? Not in the least, once one understands—or takes the trouble to understand—their ways! We Americans, however, are prone not to take such trouble. As an old Senator once said to me, "It ain't important for *us* to understand *them*. The question is do *they* understand *us!*" He was from Alabama, however.

As is the landscape of China, from the lush rice fields of South of the River to the wheat fields of North of the River, so is the food. Generally speaking, rice is the staple in the south, and wheat is the staple in the north. The North of the River folk therefore eat bread—delicious bread, noodles, buns stuffed with meats, ravioli, which Marco Polo took from China to his native Italy, bread baked, steamed, deep-fried in vegetable oils, cakes, dumplings—every imaginable way of using wheat. Millet is used, too, in the north, where it is call *siao-mi,* or "small rice."

One finds every variety of food in China, but each province, indeed each city, town, and even village has its gourmet food specialty. My hometown, Chinkiang, in the central province of Kiangsu, was justly famous for its finely cured hams. The Chinese pig is black, bristly, short-legged, and quick-tempered. Every farm family keeps a pig, perhaps two, and a few chickens; in the south a water buffalo, in the north a yellow cow. The farm families I knew—and they were many in both north and south—were contented, well-fed, hard-working, humorous, and cheerful. Their food was simple. Like Chinese food everywhere, it grew from native soil and climate. One ate the dishes the area naturally produced. The finest oranges and citrus fruits in the world are in the northern province of Fukien. The best wine comes from Shaoshing. Every farm, except in the desert-dry plains of the north, has its own fish-producing pond, but the river fish, particularly of the Yangtse, are the best. Chinese prefer fresh-water fish and crab to those of salt water. The *li* fish is a river fish and it is superb in texture and flavor, surpassing any fish I have ever tasted elsewhere in the world.

I attribute the fine foods of China to three factors: One, their ingredients are locally raised and are the products of local soil, water, and weather. They are eaten immediately and are not transported long distances. The persimmons of Peking, for example, and the pears, are delicious in texture and taste. The second factor is that food is cooked quickly. The reason for this is practical. The main fuel is grass, which makes a very hot fire but not a lasting one. There is no such thing as long boiling and simmering. Fowl, such as Peking duck, is subject to roasting over charcoal. Third, Chinese food is delicious because in China it is not frozen. Freezing is useful here in the United States, and it is the best method of preservation, but the gourmet taste of the Chinese people convinces them that the finest flavor of any food is destroyed by freezing. I remember that my friends Lin Yutang and his

All reports from China today seem to indicate an abundance of food. There were, it appears, certain years when this was not true, but with the harnessing of such willful rivers as the Yellow River, famines seem to be an event of the past. I myself am no judge of the situation, for in the regions where I grew or lived in later years there was never any scarcity of food, nor did I see scarcity in my travels north and south and to some distance westward. Everywhere I saw well-fed people, markets of greater variety in fish, game, meat, fowl, fresh fruits and vegetables than I have ever seen in any American supermarkets. Indeed, I always harbored a secret resentment of missionaries who pleaded for "the poor Chinese," because I never saw real poverty until I went to India. The rivers did overflow now and then, and fields flooded temporarily, and we had refugees from certain areas.

All this, however, does not decrease my pleasure in knowing that there is now, also, a continuing abundance of food for the Chinese people. Certainly this glimpse of a canteen in a Peking factory affirms the good news. The white-clad, white-capped man behind the counter is new, bless him, whatever gods there be in New China! I suppose only Mao Tse-tung? Well, then, bless *him!*

wife were politely grateful for a large turkey I sent them one Christmas, a turkey from my own farm, but it had been frozen for a week or two pending delivery, and though they ate the handsome bird on the appropriate day, it was with condescension, for they remarked that it was a pity such an excellent tender-fleshed bird had lost its finest flavor because of the freezing.

The preparation of food is an art in the estimate of the Chinese. They are the world's connoisseurs in selecting food before it is cooked and then in cooking it and finally in eating it. It is good manners in China to call for the cook and give him appropriate praise or suggestions for improvement should he not deserve praise. This unprejudiced criticism is appreciated by both host and cook.

V

How warmly I remember the children of China! I have seen children in many countries and in the homes of rich and poor, but the Chinese children seemed to be the happiest of all, the most joyous, the most free. A family's good fortune was measured by the number of children they had. I never knew a Chinese family without children. If a woman visitor to my home had no child of her own, she borrowed a child of a neighbor rather than appear childless. To my questions she answered so vaguely that I could not be sure whether the child was or was not hers and only further acquaintance gave the true answer. Children were treasures. Children belonged to everyone.

Of course, practically speaking, boys were more valuable than girls. Girls grew up to be women and were given away in marriage to men of other families and therefore were impermanent. The family name and prestige depended on sons. The result of this was that boys were out-rageously spoiled by all the members of the family, whereas girls ac-

Here is a stilt show in Peking. It is part of the Sien Chiao bazaar. Stilt-walking is a very old amusement in China. I can remember taking part in it myself with my Chinese playmates. Of course, our stilts were not so tall as the ones being used by these professional showmen and stilt-walkers.

There is a modern touch here, too. Three of the stilt-walkers are men. The fourth is a girl. When a man stilt-walker approaches her, he tries to kiss her. But she gives him a blow and fights him off—at least temporarily!

cepted their position and had to manage for themselves and the boys. This was and to a large extent still is the situation in Asian countries. The result is that Asian women are strong, self-disciplined, practical, inscrutable, and generally unscrupulous. When Communism came into China they were given and accepted equality as a matter of course. They had always done most of the work of everyday life and expected to continue to do so. Practically speaking again, there has always been equality between men and women in China. They had their different spheres, but they functioned equally. Chinese women received the political vote in modern China before American women in the United States received theirs.

Nominally, men ranked higher than women in China but in actuality they did not. The man had more freedom than the woman—as an example, he could have more than one wife if he could afford this luxury, but a woman could not have more than one husband. She could and did, however, consider that these secondary wives were her subordinates, indeed, almost servants, and the children they had were her legal children and this even to the extent of calling her "Mother" and their true mothers "Auntie."

Whatever the family structure and however many the wives, children were the desirable result of the family life and I never heard of birth control in China before Communism. Even under Communism it has been a fairly recent idea, and variable. For a time Mao Tse-tung himself was not in favor of it. The position of children has not changed however. The child is still treasured, even though the Pill is free and in common use in China nowadays.

Reflecting upon this, I believe that birth control in China is not so much against overpopulation as it is to maintain the total labor force. It takes time to have a child and a pregnant woman must be given time off. This means a shortage of workers and the Chinese are determined to accomplish so much, so fast, that everyone is needed. It goes without saying that women there work exactly as men do, in the heaviest sort of labor. They have always done so in China. There is nothing, literally, a man does there that a woman does not do also, except bear children. Young people are encouraged nowadays not to marry before they are in their mid-twenties and after marriage not to have more than two children.

This makes children even more precious than they were before. They are pampered and loved and they are not punished with physical force. Until a Chinese child is seven, he is allowed a total freedom. He may be as naughty as he likes, have tantrums, cry, et cetera. He does not have as much reason to do so as an American child, however, since he is never crossed or shouted at. It is expected that he will not be reasonable until he is seven. After that a gentle pressure is put upon him in the way of encouragement and praise and expectation. This pressure is general family pressure and it increases as he grows older.

For a time under the Communist desire to break up the strong family unit, elders too old to work were put in old people's homes, and children at the age of three were taken from their families and put into children's homes. The purpose of this was manifold: The women could devote themselves to labor outside the home; the children could be indoctrinated early into Communist theory. It was found, however, that the death rate for the children in the state-controlled homes was inordinately high, and so the policy now, I am told, is to allow the children to remain with their families and have the grandparents there to care for them. Every attention is paid to the child by the state, however, in day-care centers and primary schools.

In pre-Communist China where I grew up, myself, the children were happy and carefree, indulged and loved. If they suffered, it was because the family suffered. True, in times of acute distress a girl child might be sold to a wealthy family as a bondmaid, a position higher than a servant, lower than a daughter. In a kindly family she was privileged, although an evil-tempered mistress might be cruel. I doubt that children are sold nowadays in China. They are, however, still being sold in such countries as Vietnam and the Philippines, especially if, like the half-American children, they have no families. I am told that half-American girls are sold as young as five to be reared as prostitutes. Boys are sold as laborers or male prostitutes. But the presence of so many young American men in seven countries of Asia, for so many years and in rotation, has shaken Asian society to its very foundations. No one

There is something very reassuring in this homelike scene. Here is an elderly couple in their peasant home. They are not poor. They are not suddenly well-to-do. How can I tell? The furniture is old and handsome. The square table is beautifully carved and highly polished. The two armchairs match the table. They are also old, solid and of valuable teakwood.

Instead of an ancient painting, a landscape or Buddha, a plump and prosperous Mao Tse-tung now gazes smilingly above the table. On a narrow shelflike wall table there are pairs of ornamental vases and utilitarian bottles. A radio adds a modern touch.

I study the old couple. Their faces are honest, kind and good-humored. It is winter and they are comfortably dressed. The woman's feet were bound when she was a little girl in keeping with the old Chinese standards of beauty.

knows the future of these half-Americans, since our own government has no policy regarding them.

It appears that in these modern times in China the girl and the boy are given equal opportunity and there is an amazing amount of freedom allowed them. I was reared in a China where boys and girls were separated at seven, generally speaking. Now young men and women walk hand in hand in public, or even with their arms about each other. It used to be that the wife was called *nei-ren*, or "inside person," meaning she managed the affairs of the house, and the husband was called *wai-ren*, or "outside person." A man never spoke publicly of his wife; she was always "the mother of my children." Today, I hear that she or he is frankly spoken of as his, or her, *ai-ren*, or "loved one." This change in nomenclature must mean a change in the relationship between men and women, husband and wife, and therefore a change in the position of the son and daughter in the family.

Indeed it must mean a change in the very being of the country, but if it is true, then it is a change for the better.

VI

"The President of the United States came knocking at our door," Chou En Lai, the Prime Minister of China, said.

At least so the newspapers reported he said. If he did not say it, I am sure he felt it and with him many other Chinese. It is not only our President who went knocking on China's door. Whether we like it or not, he took all Americans with him. A strange turn of the world! Years ago—how many years ago was it? It seems an aeon—the American Secretary of State announced, via the newspapers, that the United States was cutting off all communications with China because a Communist government was in control there. The United Nations was at that moment having its first and preliminary meeting in San Francisco. I am of a philosophical nature, not easily moved by the unexpected, but that day my calm was shaken to the depths. Not to speak to China, when we had been, or so her people thought, her best friend for a century! Not to speak to China at a time, and through coming decades,

T'ien An Men Square, or Gate of Heavenly Peace Square, and this is the annual May Day Parade. The huge pictures of Lenin and Stalin—they were in color—on the sides of the high buildings indicate this parade took place before the Cultural Revolution. Sometimes these parades are military, but on this day it was not, I am glad to say, for it gives us a chance to see the faces of the people. I have studied them as closely as I can, even under a magnifying glass, trying to fathom the difference in these faces and the faces of the Chinese I used to know.

There are differences. I do not see old faces here. They are handsome faces, but they do not seem happy faces.

At least the crowd is well clothed and well fed. Perhaps, after all, that is enough. Perhaps it is even happiness nowadays.

crucial in human history, and this when we, out of our relationship with China, might use our influence with policies there! Indeed, lives might have been saved within China, the Korean War prevented, and certainly the war in Vietnam—or so I believe—had we not suddenly cut ourselves off from China that day.

We Americans are an emotional people, however. We are guided by feelings of sudden anger, by unreasoning prejudices. Perhaps we are too young to be philosophical, too young to take the long view. We act from the moment's impulse and at the moment. Our very American President today has so acted. He has boldly knocked at China's door. China agreed to let him in briefly, making it clear, at the same time, that Americans are expected to get out of Asia, gun, ship, plane, and man. The visit was short—Peking, Shanghai, Hangchow. The President and his entourage did not see much of China.

Has any important result come from the Presidential visit? I doubt it. Nevertheless, it has probably done no harm, either. We can even survive Chinese condescension and the position of superiority we acknowledge by "knocking on their door," because we are still the richest and most powerful nation on earth. The Chinese are the oldest and wisest, however, and there is nothing that they need from us. Their position is exactly what it was in the days of Queen Victoria when England, in her time, came knocking at China's door in the person of Lord MacCartney and an impressive entourage. The Chinese politely but firmly told him that they had no need of anything, since they had everything and, besides, knew how to make whatever they might want to have. In effect, that is what they are saying today. Self-sufficiency has always been their policy and their watchword. The trade which American businessmen are eager to establish will be disappointing. Meanwhile there remains the embarrassing, insistent demand that we Americans leave Asia and go home.

There will, of course, also be pleasant and diverting effects from President Nixon's visit. It is already the "in" thing to go to China. Today's newspaper informs me that a ship is leaving a French port for a cruise to China. There are a thousand passengers aboard, many of them Americans. They will go to China and if they are lucky they may see Peking, Shanghai, and Hangchow, but probably only Canton, which is convenient to Hong Kong. But this is a beginning and I am all for it. I hope we will be as generous about letting Chinese visit New York, Washington, and San Francisco.

The Chinese delegates at the United Nations seem greatly pleased with the attention they have been getting on the streets of New York. They are touched and amused that even couturiers are introducing Chinese styles for Westerners, especially that we have adopted the Chinese work-day pants and jacket suits that Mao Tse-tung advises as the most useful and economical outfit for honest laborers. Indeed he wears it himself at all times, at least in public. But the Chinese are not really surprised at our sudden interest in their costume and their way of life. They have always known their own superiority. Nothing surprises them, after all these thousands of years. And being so old, they are easily amused.

As for my own opinion, secret until now, of the behavior of the Chinese delegates at the United Nations this year, it is that they are so damnably clever that I have to love them in spite of their politics. Of course, they have been smiling, polite, charming, and so on, after their first firm, unequivocal confirmation of Chou En-lai's statement that we Americans must get out of Asia. Once that was over, they have proceeded to move gently and relentlessly toward leadership by cultivating the small nations who make up most of the United Nations. This they began by drinking tea—Chinese tea—in the lounge where the delegates from small nations are wont to gather. The small nations were surprised, pleased, and flattered by such notice from the largest country in the world, for they have been habitually ignored by the delegates from the United States and the Soviet Union, who are always busy with their own important affairs. The delegates were therefore wholeheartedly grateful to the Chinese, who as usual appeared benign and at ease. I need not comment further except to recall that in a congregation of states, a vote is a vote, be the state large or small. That, doubtless, is one of my Chinese memories.

Taiwan is a large island off the southeastern coast of China. It is inhabited by people who, generally speaking, are Chinese. Their his-

The Chinese have always loved pandas. And who does not? These affectionate, friendly little animals seem to have semi-human appeal. Here a baby panda is being spoon-fed by a solicitous attendant in the Peking Zoo.

tory through the centuries has been so changeful, however, that, in order to be on the safe side, they speak of themselves as Taiwanese rather than Chinese, and one can make what he likes of that.

The island, sizable and with a landscape that varies from mountain ranges to a circumference of seacoast, was "discovered" centuries ago—was it the sixteenth?—by energetic Portuguese traders, who named it Formosa, "beautiful," because of its gorgeous flowers. The Chinese, of course, had taken it for granted centuries earlier that it belonged to them, but this meant nothing to young Western nations who, if they arrived at a place they had never seen before, announced that they had "discovered" it and therefore could and did lay claim to it. Columbus behaved in the same manner toward the continent called North America, and he was followed by other Europeans and Englishmen.

China paid no heed to this invasion of Taiwan and in due course rid herself of the Portuguese. Later the island was the refuge of the last Ming Dynasty Emperor in flight from invading Manchus, and of Chiang Kai-shek fleeing from the Chinese Communists. Between these two classic retreats, however, the island was seized and held for decades by Japan. With their usual energy, Japanese built roads, opened schools, set up business, and so forth. The Taiwanese did not like the Japanese but admit that in many ways they brought in modern improvements.

Certainly they preferred the efficient Japanese to the first Chinese general whom Chiang Kai-shek sent to Taiwan to reclaim it after the Japanese had surrendered and the Second World War ended. This general, apparently unaware of modern times, behaved in the traditional manner of old-fashioned Chinese warlords and despoiled the land and people of Taiwan to such extent that they declared openly that they preferred the former Japanese rulers to the present Chinese. Chiang Kai-shek changed this when he himself took over, but there remained some sentiments made privately and confidentially in safe places and behind locked doors. In the open the Taiwanese say they would like to be independent, pointing out that there are many nations, now sitting in the United Nations, which are smaller, numerically, than they are.

There is not the slightest chance, however, that they will be given such independence. The Chinese people do not think of time in years, as we Americans do. They think of time as eternity, divided into small units called centuries. Since Taiwan belonged in eternity to China, she still belongs to China. All that has happened in the last centuries is momentary, transient, immaterial. The only question now in the re-establishment of the old union is how it will be done.

The answer is simple enough. The Chinese will do it. It is an internal matter and no foreign government or person need even inquire. It will simply be done, accomplished, announced, and this not in head-lines. It is not important. There may be an interval until death removes two old leaders, yet there may be no interval. For all any Westerner knows, since it is not our business, arrangements may already have been made. Certainly whispers were brought to my ears during the Eisenhower regime that Chiang Kai-shek had been offered an "honor-able retirement" in Peking and safety for all concerned if Taiwan voluntarily returned to where she belonged as part of China proper. Whispers said that Chiang asked the advice of an important American official then visiting Taiwan who vehemently declared that the invita-tion must be vigorously declined and that the United States would support Nationalist China "to the death"—whatever that means. At that time Chiang Kai-shek believed the American and therefore de-clined the Chinese Communist overture.

Whispers not withstanding, the fact is that the present Chinese dele-gation to the United Nations represents all China, and this, from their point of view, includes Taiwan. And if Taiwan does not protest, who can deny the assumption? Was there discussion on this matter of Tai-wan when President Nixon went to Peking? I doubt it, unless he insisted. If he did insist, his remarks would have been courteously brushed aside by other remarks as to whether his tea was still hot, and how fortunate it was that the weather was so fine, a good omen indeed in this Year of the Rat, and would he let them know the date when he planned to remove all Americans, ships, and military planes from Asia, and so forth.

The Year of the Rat, 1972 in the West, is 4670 in China, and the

The solitary figure in this scene is a commune worker. The commune is the Shu Kwang, or Rising Sun Commune, in the Wuhan area in Central China. It is a rice-growing area. The grain has been winnowed and the worker is sweeping the threshing floor. The straw is in stacks, very much as peasants in France stack their straw and hay. Not only rice is grown in this area of the Rising Sun Commune but also wheat. The Commune, or Cooperative, if one prefers, also has five industrial and scientific centers; one is for agricultural machinery; another for transport, others for scientific research with twelve peasant researchers, and an experimental laboratory doing research for the transformation of chemicals in body wastes into electric power.

As always, the human being interests me most. This worker shields himself from the heat of the sun by a farmer's hat of woven bamboo strips. He does not wear the Mao costume, but the usual peasant garb of loose trousers of black cotton reaching to the calf of the leg. His jacket or tunic is probably of faded blue cotton cloth. It is girdled about his waist with a strip of coarse unbleached white cotton. He wears straw sandals, which he makes at home, perhaps in the winter. He is reasonably honest, he is hard-working, shrewd and basically bewildered by life in general but specifically about the government, whatever it is—God bless him! It is a common affliction.

Chinese New Year's Day is on February the fifteenth of our year. The Year of the Rat is always a lucky year for international affairs. By the way, if a Westerner has a dislike for rats, he may also call it the Year of the Mouse. This is the first year in a new cycle of years, or as Westerners would say, a new era. In general, the year is not a brilliant one, the rat—or mouse—being in general a timid and furtive creature. Certainly it is not a good year for marriage and no sensible Chinese would plan for marriage this year.

Summing up our present situation in the Year of the Rat, on the whole I feel optimistic, not because of any event past, present, or likely to come in the immediate future. I am optimistic because now we all know each other better nationally than we did before the President made his dramatic visit to China. Other nations now know that we are impulsive, dramatic, and that we are still very young and immature. We think of ourselves and act without considering what the results will be in other parts of the world. Therefore we are not to be trusted. No, perhaps that is too harsh. Let us say we are not to be counted on and therefore even our friends must not put all their eggs in our basket.

And we? Have we learned anything? A little, perhaps, and it may be more than I think. We learned something when at the opening of the United Nations in 1971 an uproar of approval followed the flat belligerence of the speech made by the chief delegate from China. We learned that we are not loved always and by everyone. When some delegates even danced in delight we were offended rather than amused. In fact, we were shocked.

Ah well, perhaps one has to be very old before one learns how to be amused rather than shocked. And the fact remains that we, the nations, really know each other better than we did before—at least a little better.

Thank you, Mr. President!

VII

I have spent most of the hours and days of my life, it seems to me, in writing and talking about China. This has been partly because China is still the country I know best and the Chinese are the people with whom I am the most familiar. The more important reason, however, is that I am appalled and oppressed by the discovery that American people are almost totally ignorant of China, nor have they any great desire to learn more about this ancient and mighty nation who will and must affect our own nation and people in the future more than any other. Even our so-called "experts" are one-sided and superficial, however sincere. There is not one of them with whom I can talk beyond superficialities. They have not the *feel* of the Chinese people. They do not belong there.

"Are you going back to China?" people ask me.

"I have never left China," I reply. "I belong to China, as a child, as a young girl, as a woman, until I die."

My friend Hu Shih said to me one day before his death, "You will live here in America but when you are very old and feel death near, you will go back so that your body will be buried in Chinese earth."

I neither denied nor affirmed. I do not know. But I love my own country so that I am strangely afraid to return to China, lest I die there —not by sudden death at human hands, but because Hu Shih might be right. Therefore, although I long to see my Chinese people and learn whether they have changed, which I cannot believe without seeing, I hardly dare go, lest I never return.

The landscape, I am sure, is the same, those great smoothly flowing rivers, the fretted seashores, the rounded southern hills, those clifflike, wind-carved mountains of the northwest, the terraced hillsides of rice-growing fields; the wide wheat fields of the north, the magnificent cities, the small homelike villages—surely these are not changed. But my friends, those with whom I grew up, the families I knew and visited and who visited me—are they still there? And if some have been allowed to live through the holocaust of revolution, could we talk of everything under heaven as once we did?

These are questions I cannot answer. Perhaps no one can answer. Yet today I feel a new eagerness. I am to have a visitor for a few days, a man—not American but Australian—who comes to me fresh from a long visit in China. Perhaps he will know. Perhaps he can answer my questions. It is an exciting day for me, a winter's day, snow on the Vermont mountains, and deep in the valleys, an ordinary day, one would say, but not for me. I am to have a visitor from China!

It behooves me to prepare for the visit of the young Australian by reviewing further China's past. Again and again I am forced to the conclusion that we cannot understand China's present unless we know her past. Moreover, the relationship of Australia to China is very different indeed from that of the United States to China. Australia is a young country—younger even than ours. She is a Western country in culture but she is a continental island in Asia—a peculiar and at times perilous and contradictory position. She has defended herself thus far by excluding Asians from landing on her shores. Now, however, with

Communism linking one country to another, defying ancient barriers, she is still in peril, a new peril.

Moreover, my visitor is a man and a young man, in comparison to my age. There is also the fact that I am a woman who has spent most of her life in China. He went to China recently and with a fresh approach. My approach to the present is always based on past experience. He cannot make comparisons. I am compelled to comparisons. Let me then consider further the great changes in the past in order to assess what I learn of the present.

Just as Buddhism entered China during the decline of the great Han dynasty, Russian Communism came into China in 1921 in a period of disturbance and political confusion. For ten years the efforts of the young Chinese revolutionists to establish a modern government, a republic based on the model of the American republic, had failed. Of course it was doomed from the start, alien as it was to Chinese history and thought. Meanwhile, in 1917, Russian Communism had succeeded in overthrowing its opponents, and the Communists in power offered aid to the helpless young Chinese revolutionists. Sun Yat-sen, their leader, unable to secure support from any other source, accepted the Russian offer, and in 1921 Communism was recognized as a political party in China.

I was in China in those days and for many years thereafter, as I have told on earlier pages. Let me only say that neither I nor my Chinese friends had any conception of what was ahead. We knew we were in a period of continuing change, but so we had been for nearly two decades. One warlord after another had come and gone. We knew there was a revolutionary group under Sun Yat-sen, but we thought he was just another contender. He had died of cancer of the liver in 1925, and none of us took his party seriously after that. True, we saw Soviet Russians everywhere, but otherwise life went on as usual until we heard of a Second Revolution forming in the south, with an army preparing to march north. We were so accustomed to warlord armies coming and going, however, that we did not take the news seriously. Work went on as usual in the universities. In the spring of 1927 I superintended the

These are familiar streets to me, for here in Nanking I lived for seventeen years and from it I and all foreigners, which included Japanese, were driven out when the army of the Second Revolution entered our city gates, after three days of bitter fighting. The American vice-president of the University of Nanking was killed, among other foreigners, that day. The Japanese were treated with special cruelty, for which Japan took special revenge when her armies conquered the city in the Second World War. In the Second Revolution the Chinese called themselves "liberators," too. The year was 1927.

Here they are again, Soldiers of the Liberation, decades later. They look the same, their faces pitifully young, harassed, bewildered. They are carrying their belongings on their shoulder poles, even the huge iron cauldrons in which their rice is cooked. They are on their way somewhere—always on their way.

This street I know. Nevertheless I doubt that now there are rickshas anymore. I think they have been replaced by bicycles and pedicabs. Probably there are also some modern buildings.

At any rate, this city, Nanking, was the capital during Chiang Kai-shek's brief and troubled rule. We all came back then and resumed our work in the universities, both American and Chinese. My home, ransacked and occupied for two years, I restored and refurnished, and we lived there again as a family, uncertain but hopeful of the future.

It was too much, however, even for the determined Chiang Kai-shek. His relentless pursuit of the Communists, his efforts to unite the warlords behind him, his attempt to create a modern democratic government of a sort new even to him, were enough in themselves. When Japan chose this hour to attack China, it was indeed too much. He was doomed, in spite of every good intention.

Yet Nanking is a city eternal in eternal China. Today, modernized, she stands firmly connected with the north by a magnificent new bridge. The Chinese made it themselves. They have every reason to be proud of it.

planting of my lovely garden, and wandered through the bamboo grove in search of young shoots, a favorite food.

Meanwhile the Second Revolutionary Army, then still under Chiang Kai-shek, was marching down the banks of the Yangtse River toward us and on the twenty-fifth—or was it the day before that?—the Battle of Nanking began. The nine city gates were barred and no one could come or go. We waited, wondering whether our old anti-revolutionary war-lord would win or if the victory would go to the young revolutionary army from the south. Three days and we knew. The gates were stormed, the revolutionary army had won, and they were Communists. An American was killed and other foreigners also that day. Others were wounded, and all were driven out of home. After two days of not knowing whether we would all be killed, we were taken out of the city, rescued by foreign warships.

What do I remember of the Chinese people on that fateful day? I remember above all a Chinese tailor who always did our sewing. He ran to us early in that morning of the twenty-seventh to tell us the victors were Communists and were killing all foreigners. The American vice-president of our university was already shot. The story of that tailor I told in my short story, "The Frill," written years later when I was safely in my own country.

I remember, too, the slender young college professor, a most valued assistant to an American department head, who risked his life again and again to come to our hiding place to tell us to remain there, that he was interceding with Communist officers for our lives. At the end of the day he came for the last time and kneeling on the earthen floor of the thatched hut where we were hidden, he begged us to forgive his country and his countrymen, for he had done all he could.

The hut? It belonged to a poor woman, a refugee from the north, who had followed me to Nanking, and that story I have also told. She saved my life that day and the lives of my family. And everywhere in the city American lives were saved by Chinese friends. Thus, few foreigners were killed except in the large Japanese community, where the Japanese were killed so ruthlessly that Japan swore vengeance, which oath she fulfilled in the Second World War, when newspaper reports in the United States told of what they called "the rape of Nanking." I was not there to see it, but I had long known what it would be when it came, for I had seen what befell the Japanese community in Nanking in 1927. On that day many Japanese were killed, men, women and children, and their homes ransacked. The whole area of the city where they had lived was emptied and ruined. The hatred of the Chinese against the Japanese had been accumulating for centuries, ever since Hidegoshi, the Japanese warrior, had dreamed of capturing China and becoming its Viceroy Emperor. Given imperial permission, he had prepared a fleet of warships and set sail across the sea westward to China. He was stopped only by the Korean warships, the "turtle ships," as they were called, for they were covered with iron, the earliest iron ships in human history. The iron was pierced with holes to allow flaming arrows to be shot at the Japanese wooden ships, which were thus set on fire. Hidegoshi yielded, and died before he even saw China.

The Chinese people were always aware of the Japanese desire to expand their meager lands, however, and they never forgot, either, the Japanese attack in 1894, nor did they fail to be aware of the encroachment of Japan in her secret negotiations with warlords, her foothold on Chinese soil after World War I. This ancient enmity between the two peoples flamed into incidents, the most serious of which was the Nanking Incident of 1927, which the Japanese swore to avenge, and did so avenge in World War II by a ruthless attack, which I have described in my novel *Dragon Seed*.

I, too, with my family, was driven from the city in 1927, and took refuge in Japan, strangely enough, never thinking then that both countries would undergo in my lifetime such violent change. Yes, in 1927 we left, not knowing whether we would ever come back.

But we did come back two years later, when Chiang Kai-shek had repudiated the Communists and had set up his new government, the National Republic of China. We came back and lived again in the same comfortable gray brick house, cleaned of its war filth and ruin and freshly painted. We lived there for a few years, uncertain years, but

This is the new bridge crossing the wide and turbulent Yangtse River at Nanking. The city itself is about seven miles away, but good modern roads connect it to the bridge and thence by rail to the "North of the River" country.

The bridge is today one of the great sights of new China. There is another great bridge connecting Hangkow and Wuhan about a thousand miles up the river. The new Chinese built that also, but with the help of Russian engineers. The bridge at Nanking, however, was built after the Chinese began quarreling with the Russians. It is therefore an engineering feat entirely their own and it proves the extraordinary and swiftly developed modern skills of the new Chinese.

The Yangtse River at Nanking—and how many times I have crossed it by old-fashioned ferry boat!—is 1,574 feet wide and 45 feet deep. The currents are tangled and swift. The approaches to the bridge on both sides are impressive and some miles long. On the Nanking side there is a People's Park and one can reach the bridge by elevator, or higher up, from the street. The elevator rises first to the train level, then the car level and pedestrian level. There are four great towers at the ends of the bridge, in which there are halls for exhibitions and art objects sent from many provinces. There is also a lecture hall with models of the bridge, photographs and architects' drawings showing how the bridge was made.

The Russians did, as a matter of fact, plan and indeed contract to help with this bridge, as they did with the one at Wuhan. But the break came between the two powers, and the Russians destroyed the contracts in 1960. Nor did they deliver the steel girders they had promised in 1959. It was a challenge to the Chinese and they accepted it heroically. The four towers were up in eighteen days, although the Russians had allowed nine months for this work. The bridge was finished in record time and finished well. The result was an enormous rise in Chinese self-confidence. They could build and manufacture without foreign aid!

The psychological, even spiritual effects of the Nanking Bridge equal its practical benefit. Perhaps these even excel, for now the Chinese are really independent. They know they can do anything —and by themselves.

peaceful from day to day, until in 1931 Japan took Manchuria, and in 1934 I saw wars ahead and left China for my own country.

I remember, forever, my Chinese home in Nanking. Though I may never see it again, I remember.

In the attic workroom of my home there my desk faced a wide window, from whence I looked across the city roofs and over the city wall, to Purple Mountain, upon whose flank is the great tomb of Sun Yat-sen. I attended his funeral in 1925 and when it had ended I climbed the flights of marble steps to the entrance hall of the tomb. It was empty, for all was over, the people gone. Suddenly a door opened and Chiang Kai-shek came out alone. He was in military uniform and a sword clanked at his heels. He did not see me and I did not speak. He strode across the marble floor and stood at the open doors and gazed across the vast landscape of hills and valleys and in the distance the city of Nanking, where he was to make his capital. I remember his eyes, large eyes for a Chinese, and burning that day like the eyes of a tiger.

When people ask me what I think of Chiang Kai-shek, I remember him as I saw him first that day and I can only answer that no one knows Chiang Kai-shek. He was never given time to show anyone what he is. I lived under his rule until I left China in 1934. By then I knew there would be another world war. Knowing Chinese history as I do, living as I did through the greatest revolution China ever had, watching Chiang Kai-shek struggling against the heaviest odds a man could have, a disrupted country, the oldest on earth and the largest in area, inhabited by the greatest population, threatened by a foreign revolution from Russia, attacked by a foreign power, Japan, all at the same time and in that short time compelled to form a new government with whose form and policies he was totally unfamiliar—who can know Chiang Kai-shek? History did not allow him time to make himself known. He knew, all during the world war in which he and his country were soon engulfed, that his real battles were still to come. He gambled on winning and toward that desperate end he maintained his own army. When he was forced to retreat to Taiwan, he took his own army with him, undefeated. Who knows Chiang Kai-shek?

"Tell me," I said to my Australian guest, "were you allowed to go to Nanking?"

He hesitated and then replied, "Yes—I was allowed—but—"

"But?" I repeated.

"It seemed the most controlled place I visited."

Controlled? I remembered it as a city beautifully free. I had wandered everywhere alone and unafraid. I remembered the summer evenings on Lotus Lake. It is a big lake—one can spend hours floating on its smooth surface, the water half hidden by huge lotus leaves and great rosy lotus flowers. In season the boatmen, if they knew you as a friend, would wrench the seed pods from under the leaves and open them to press out the pearl-colored seeds, each as big as a marble and sweet to the taste. There was a concession on the lotus seeds and no one was supposed to pluck them, but a friend was always a friend in the days of that China.

"Yes," the Australian said, "I was taken for a boatride—only it's not called Lotus Lake now. I didn't see any lotus—perhaps it wasn't the season."

Memories crowded my mind. I was able to see the ancient beautiful Drum Tower from my attic window. It was really a huge ceremonial gate through which emperors used to come and go, and its walls were washed an imperial red.

"Is the Drum Tower still there?" I asked.

He hesitated again before he answered. "Yes, but they wouldn't let me go through it—though finally, when I urged, they let me go through the back. When I saw the front finally, it seemed to be closed."

"Did they show you the Porcelain Pagoda?" I asked.

The Porcelain Pagoda had been one of the show places of old Nanking. In it was a bell of unusually melodious tone, haunting in its quality. Some said it was because of the porcelain tiles of which the pagoda was built. The old legend, however, was that the bellmaker, the most famous in all of China, could not make the metal mold into the quality he sought. In a dream he was told that until his three beautiful daughters, all virgins, threw themselves into the molten metal, the bell would crack as it cooled. When he told his daughters of his dream, they resolved secretly to sacrifice themselves. They did so, and though the bellmaker's heart was broken, the bell was created in perfection, its tone forever haunting in its beauty.

Forever? I put my memories away.

Then he added, as if he had just remembered, "They did take me to Purple Mountain to see Sun Yat-sen's tomb. It is very well cared for."

Yes, I remembered that view!

"And did they show you the old Ming Tombs, and did you walk up the avenue of huge old marble statues?"

He shook his head. "Nothing was said about Ming Tombs."

"And the fine old Buddhist temple halfway up the mountain!"

"No Buddhist temple."

On a summer's day I had rested in that temple, had received tea and little sesame cakes from the gentle monks, and thus refreshed, I had climbed to the top of the mountain. Then I had looked over the other side. It was blue, from my feet to the valley far below, sky blue, with wild lupine in flower.

There were many questions to put to my Australian visitor. He had as many to put to me. We had the same intention, which was to learn as much as we could from each other concerning China, he of the past, I of the present, in order that we might make comparisons. He had, it seemed, been allowed more freedom, though this within limitations, than he had expected. He had objected to being taken everywhere by car and accompanied by a Chinese, but it was possible to insist upon walking and proceeding to do so. This determination made him leave his quarters alone occasionally and walk when he wished. He reported that the people looked clean, well fed, and reasonably content. He speaks Chinese Mandarin and was able to understand certain discontents also. Certainly the Chinese are under controls. The old free individualism is gone, but so, apparently, have extreme wealth and extreme poverty. There are variations, nevertheless, and the inevitable corruptions of bureaucracy are creeping in.

He saw no actual suffering, but there was little emphasis on beauty. I remarked that the average Chinese never did find beauty essential to his surroundings. This was and is very different from the life-style of Japan, where some touch of beauty is found even in the poorest house. Beauty in China was associated with wealth. I remember thinking much about this even when I was very young and wondering why this was so. The Chinese were—and I suppose are—healthy, earthy, humor-loving, gay, but they can live without beauty. I cannot, for to me life without beauty, however scanty my purse, is spiritual death. My thoughts on this were expressed long ago in the second article I ever wrote, an article published in an American magazine now defunct. The article was entitled "Beauty in China." I remember concluding that the average Chinese felt no need to expend money on an object of beauty because beauty was everywhere about him in landscape. Yet when he became rich he bought objects of beauty and built a house of great beauty, if it were of Chinese design and architecture. His clothes, if Chinese, were of exquisite silks and brocaded satins. I gather, however, that there is now a certain monotony in costume for the Chinese, though brighter colors are creeping in and young women are daring a little jewelry. In my time all women enjoyed rings and earrings and silver and even gold and jade hair ornaments, and flowers in their hair, especially gardenias.

How often on a summer's day when I lived in Nanking did I look from my bedroom window, before I was dressed for the day, only to see my Chinese women neighbors, poor women from a little cluster of huts outside the wall, come stealing through the back gate to pick fragrant gardenia blossoms from my gardenia bushes! I never let them know I saw them or that I missed a flower, for I knew their special enjoyment of the scent and beauty of gardenias. Nor did any woman take more than one, which she thrust into her chignon of black hair, to enjoy the day through.

Yet Chinese villages were never like the villages of Japan, where every house has its bit of landscape garden, a rock, a crooked tree, a few feet of pebbled walk, and in the main room inside the house, however humble, there is an alcove, a small shelf, some little place, where there is a flower, a picture, or perhaps only a green pine branch. This difference typifies, perhaps, the essential difference in the countries—

Japan, small and exquisite in detail; China, huge and various in its immense landscapes.

I doubt there is much thought for beauty in today's China. The rich are no more and those who were low yesterday are high today. The so-called cultural revolution put an end, at least for untold time to come, for the elite of the past, those who had the education, the time and the means for the cultivation of beauty. Today I read the account of an American's recent visit to the People's Republic of China:

> Our hostess told us that there had been many changes in the kindergarten since "the great proletarian cultural revolution."
>
> "Before the teachers and revolutionary workers here answered Chairman Mao's great call to overthrow the reactionary line of the traitor Liu Shao-chi and reform education, there were many bad things at our kindergarten," she said.
>
> She told us previously that children had been proud and arrogant simply because they were at school; time was wasted teaching trivial songs and fairy tales. Now, however, things were different. As we toured the building and grounds we saw one room with little tables and chairs where the children were working on handicrafts.
>
> "Before the cultural revolution the children wasted their time and accomplished nothing. Now they are engaged in production," she explained.
>
> They were busily engaged making small boxes out of their cardboard. The boxes would be sent to a local medical center to hold bottles of medication.
>
> At the back of the school buildings was a small garden which the older children were responsible for maintaining. Instead of simply being told how to plant and tend vegetables, they have the opportunity to learn by doing. This blending of theory and practical experience characterizes China's entire educational system.*

Beauty, of course, is deathless. It is essential for the human spirit. Without it, the human fiber coarsens and the creative mind is stifled, thereby killing the soul of the being. I do not doubt that beauty exists in China as it always has. If today it is not acknowledged as necessary, it is recognized secretly by human beings who keep silent until they dare to speak. In silence beauty is cherished.

* Charles Mossop, Special to *The Christian Science Monitor,* April 22, 1972.

And here I remember my Chinese friend who visited me not long ago. She is—or was—a brilliant pianist, graduate of Juilliard, a performer of the first rank. Seeking to serve her country, she returned and did indeed develop some promising pianists. Her own hands, however, were knotted and gnarled by the hours she was compelled each day to devote to hard labor. Here in my living room she endeavored to play a favorite sonata by Beethoven. Alas, she could not. Those beautiful hands, once so in the art of lovely music, could perform no more. She bowed her head and the tears came.

"I can no longer make music," she mourned.

For a time, for a time, the people in China must be punished for the sins of the past, when indeed beauty was the possession of the few. Today other lessons must be taught, I suppose, and ancient wrongs be righted. But beauty is the phoenix. It cannot be buried forever, nor forever forbidden. The day will come when, out of sheer spiritual necessity, people will seek beauty for the comfort, the joy, the inspiration of their souls. And seeking, they will find, in their own necessity to create that which they do most deeply desire.

We discussed every phase of Chinese life, the Australian and I, and exchanged and compared, and at last I asked a question that had hung about in the corners of my mind for a long time.

"Tell me what they told you about the recovery of Tibet," I said. "Did you ask them questions?"

He reflected a moment and then smiled a small half-bitter smile. "It was my impression that they are half ashamed of it," he said.

I pressed no further about Tibet. I have my own sources of information on that subject and my own mixed feelings—mixed because I knew the old Chinese point of view firsthand and the present Tibetan point of view, also firsthand. Let me give the Chinese view first, for with that view I grew up. After China was old enough and mature enough to understand the uselessness of aggressive war, she rejected it even for defensive purposes. Instead, her people adopted two methods of self-defense. The first was to absorb invaders into their own culture and population. The second was to surround their country with smaller, friendly nations who paid tribute to the Emperor in return for which

A student group, again at work on manual labor, here cultivates their "own" farm. They are students of Wuhan University, in Central China. They have flooded a rice field, preparatory to planting the rice seedlings which are in a seedbed. The soil must be spaded up and softened. It is clear they are not peasants. Not one of them handles his spade properly. Moreover, it is doubtful that a spade is the proper instrument. I grew up in rice-growing country in Central China and I never saw a field thus prepared for rice seedlings. The field was plowed by a plow drawn by a slow-moving water buffalo. Behind him, trousers rolled up, walked the farmer, guiding the plow. There was no such feverish activity as this. It is clear, then, these are intellectuals, university students, and certainly not peasants. I fear they do not know what they are doing agriculturally. Never mind! At any event, they are obeying their government and Mao Tse-tung.

he would send a volunteer army if and when they were attacked by other nations. Tibet was such a nation, so was Korea, and so were Indo-China, Nepal, Ladokh, Bhutan, and Sikkim. Thus when the United Nations forces entered Korea it was to be expected, by anyone who knew Chinese history and understood the Chinese point of view, that China would send a "volunteer army" into Korea. This was not, as I have said previously, an "actual aggression," although it was so declared by persons who did not know Chinese history or understand her point of view.

Tibet, however, had been attacked by China under the guise of "protection," and since I was in India soon after the Dalai Lama and many of his people had escaped the attack by the long march over the Himalayas, I had been able to talk with him as well as with members of his family. I had also visited Tibetan refugee camps in Mussoorie, Darjeeling, Kalimpong, and elsewhere, and it was impossible not to believe the stories told me of ferocious behavior on the part of the Chinese. Something new had come into China. Socialism had, as I have written, been tried again and again in her past, but this was more than socialism. It was revolutionary aggression. The tactics of Chinese persuasion had changed. The core of Communism is the theory that the end justifies the means. If the Chinese have adopted this as their faith, then China is changed indeed and the Chinese are a changed people. This is what I must discover—whether they are changed, and if so how permanently.

Knowing only the present, the young Australian could not help me. I must return to my own sources, and they must be Chinese sources.

I have had no personal connections with anyone in China since Communism took over that country, with the exception of one or perhaps two letters from a Chinese friend who was returned to China by U. S. Immigration officials. I answered neither of these letters. It is not that I have forgotten my friends in China, and I am sure they have not forgotten me. It is simply that I do not wish to endanger their lives or make trouble for myself, either. I do have many Chinese friends in the United States, however, who prefer to remain here. Yet they have families in China, parents and brothers and sisters and other relatives with whom they keep in touch in various ways and by various means, and from them I glean some information.

I gather that nothing has disturbed and even shocked the Chinese people so deeply and perhaps permanently as the youth movement called the Cultural Revolution. It is over now, but only recently, and its effects will last for a long time—perhaps forever. It began formally in the summer of 1966. The most prominent instigator and leader seems to have been Chiang Ching, the wife of Mao Tse-tung, but other leaders took part in the opening speeches broadcast all over China to young students in their preparatory schools and colleges. Some word had spread about earlier but only when the government officials themselves announced it did the movement begin to work. Chiang Ching in an opening speech declared that there were persons who were pretending to support the Red government but were secretly plotting its downfall. Therefore a new revolution, "The Great Socialist Cultural Revolution," must be undertaken by the youth of China. Their duty was to destroy "the four Olds—old thoughts, old culture, old customs, old habits."

In effect, this meant the youth were to destroy Chinese civilization. Chou En-lai himself gave instructions as to how the Cultural Revolution was to be carried out. Universities, middle schools, and technical schools were to be closed in order that all students above the primary school stage could devote their time and energy to the new revolution. The first- and second-year students in junior middle schools could attend classes in the mornings and give their afternoons to the movement.

The first task of the students thus released from classes was to attack their teachers and charge them with being "revisionists," or persons who secretly wished to return to the old ways and culture. The attacks in posters and newspapers were mild indeed in comparison to what followed. Students were allowed, even encouraged, to follow attacks, trials, judgments, by cruel punishments. Teachers were beaten, tortured, forced to eat insects and excrement, hung by their arms and legs, compelled to kneel on broken glass; and other cruelties beyond description were committed. The students were joined by others who

In a Peking hospital a Chinese doctor, carefully uniformed in the most modern Western hygienic manner, administers ancient acupuncture to a little girl. She submits but obviously with some anxiety. Acupuncture is a technique that has been known to me, of course, throughout my life. I have seen it used with apparent success since earliest memory. Its fallacy, until now, was that infections were common because needles were not sterilized between patients. It was strange that the germ theory was not known to Chinese doctors or even accepted until China became acquainted with its validity through Western education. Now, however, with sterilization taken as a matter of course by modern Chinese surgeons and doctors, acupuncture can be scientifically tested for its actual value. Even so, there will be patients, at least in the West, who will share this little Chinese girl's concern as she watches the needle thrust into her tender flesh.

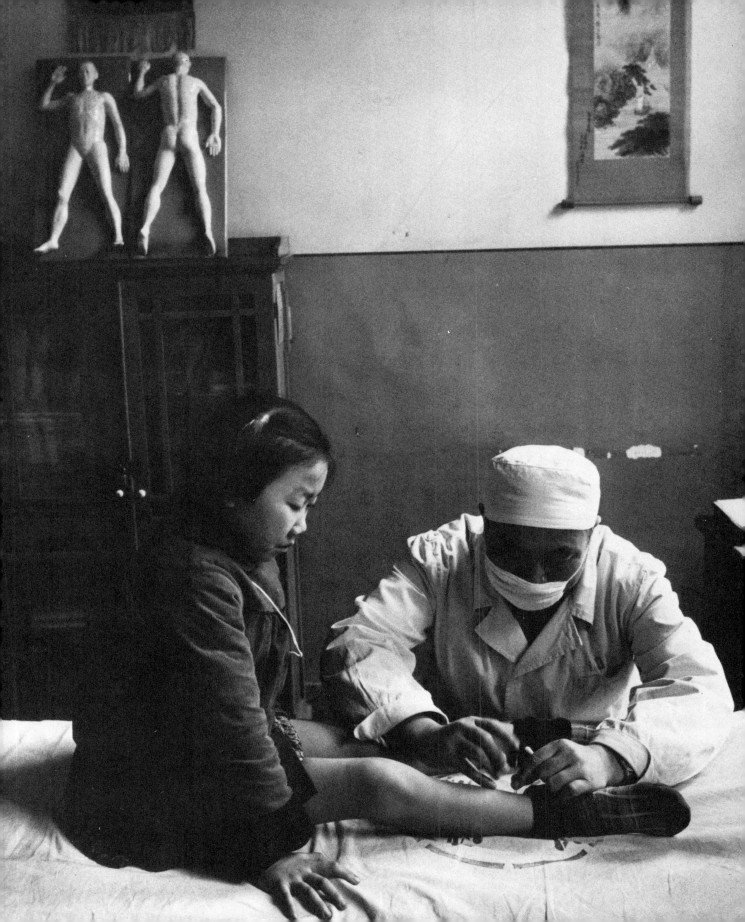

This scene could be taken from an American television series. It is not in the United States, however. It was photographed in a modern Chinese hospital in Wuhan, a great metropolitan area in Central China.

The patient, a Chinese woman, is having a tumor removed. She is conscious; she is eating slices of fruit put in her mouth by a medical assistant; she feels no pain under the surgeon's knife although she has not been given an anaesthetic. Instead she is anaesthetized by acupuncture.

It is not surprising that Western scientists, doctors and surgeons are deeply interested in acupuncture. There are many questions to be answered and much sound study to be made before it can be wholly accepted. Some Americans in China have allowed it to be used on themselves. I cannot speak from personal experience for I have never had it used on me. But it is interesting, even exciting, to watch a technique centuries old and familiar to me since earliest childhood tested now by the most severe scientific standards.

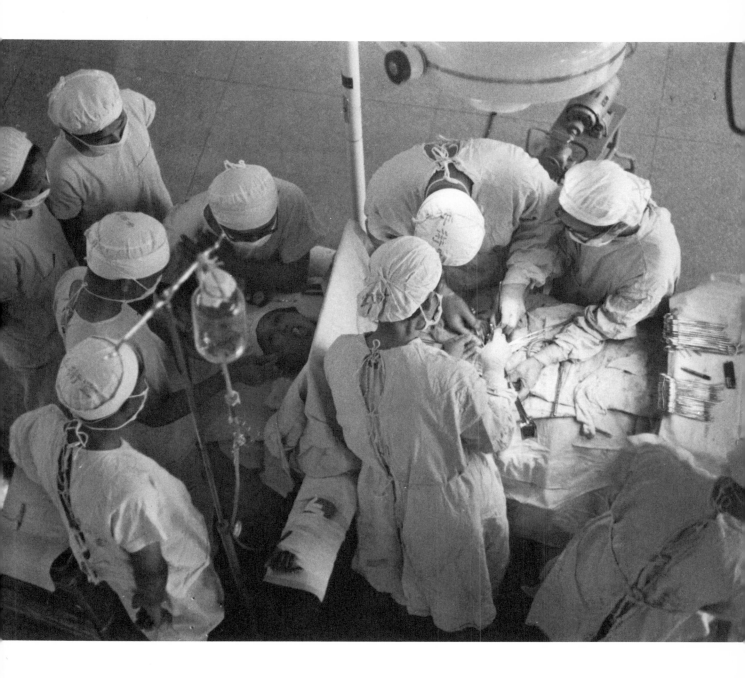

had failed in school and thus were filled with hate and resentment against their former teachers. Children or peasants, untutored and coarse, joined in the destruction of schools and ancient buildings of culture. *The young people, both male and female, were known as the Red Guards. It was a cultural revolution, as Chiang Ching said, without precedent in history.

I need not elaborate here upon its shocking and tragic course—shocking because of the irreparable damage it did to places and buildings of historic beauty and, worse than that, the suffering and sorrow it brought to China's finest teachers and professors, some of whom lost their lives in degrading torture; and tragic because the youth of China were led so far astray as to disgrace and betray their country in the eyes of the civilized world, who for centuries had looked to China as the highest center of culture in human history.

The attack on teachers was peculiarly significant because the teacher, the scholar, the man of learning, composed the highest and most honored and honorable class in Chinese history. To dishonor them was indeed to cast the final dishonor upon Confucius himself, who, five hundred years before the Christian era, had defined the superior man. For centuries teachers had been honored by their students and indeed by all citizens. When a child first went to school, his parents presented him with a ceremony to his teacher, and the teacher accepted the responsibility of moral as well as mental education.

The question may well be asked why Communist students were therefore encouraged to disgrace their teachers and attack them with false accusations and actual torture and in some cases death. The only answer that I have been given is that it was true that these intelligent, cultivated, and moral men saw the flaws in the new regime and did indeed long for a return to the civilization they knew and revered. There was also a danger that in their teaching they might reveal the flaws, injustices, and weaknesses in the new regime. It was a clever political move therefore to turn students who knew nothing of the past against those who knew and remembered.

* See Ken Ling, *The Revenge of Heaven, The Journal of a Young Chinese* (New York: G. P. Putnam's Sons, 1972).

The real tragedy of the Cultural Revolution, however, was the betrayal of the young people, the corruption of their minds. They were deprived of their glorious heritage, the magnificent civilization of their own country. It was true that in the decline of a dynasty, in the overthrow of the traditional form of government, a disturbed interval always took place. This had happened before in China's long history but the times had righted themselves because the basic patterns of government remained firm. In this generation, however, the basic pattern was destroyed. The very foundations of China's civilization were attacked. What had been the moral order was decried. The consequence was a generation of confused young people who, obeying their leaders, committed crimes and even atrocities under the impression that what they were doing was right. They realized at last, many of them and the most intelligent, how cruelly they had been misled. I quote from Ken Ling's diary:

What I thought of most constantly now was returning to school, to classroom 1-5 and sitting in my old seat, the seventh in the third row. I would put my head down and think. Could I—the Red Guard who had risen so high—really go back and obey the old classroom rules? Could I ever reinstate my respect for the teachers so humiliated by us under struggle? . . . When I thought of the empty seat in this room one day when school would open, I wanted to jump out of the window and kill myself.

Many of my colleagues spoke frequently of escaping to Hong Kong. "If only," they would say, "there were a road leading to Hong Kong, we would go, even if we had to crawl all the way." . . . It was not Hong Kong, however, that Second Brother had in mind when I—a leader without responsibilities and a student without studies—went to him one day in April to tell him that I was ready to escape with him. In his thorough fashion he had consulted both maps and calendars on the moon and tides and had made his decision. We would escape by swimming to Tatan Island, off the shore of Quemoy.

. . . On July 19, 1968 I awoke at five o'clock in the morning. In the sky there were small patches of cloud, pierced by the rays of the rising sun. It was going to be a still, hot and sunny day—a good omen . . . When Mother went out on an errand, I rushed to dispose of the belongings in my room . . . Then, piling up all my diaries of the last eight years, I set them afire. Before striking the match, I turned to the first page of the first

Another commune scene, and this was taken at a time when something over ninety percent of China's peasants were in communes. This is a busy scene and most of the workers are students, thus carrying out Mao Tse-tung's principle that intellectuals must share the manual labor of the peasants. I do not know whether the converse of this principle is also practiced.

At any rate, there seem to be only two real peasants in this scene—the farmer, wearing a peasant hat, and examining a cabbage. The other peasant is a woman, perhaps the farmer's wife. She holds a basket. On her head is the piece of cloth worn by most peasant women in Central and North China. She wears black cotton trousers and a white jacket, standard peasant wear for women. I take it that this scene is in North China since the cabbages are of the northern or Shantung variety. The worm-eaten outer leaves of the cabbages are being stripped off, leaving the clean, hard inner core. The baskets are of woven willow withes and split bamboo. The young people are working with such zeal that I am sure they are students inspired by Maoism. The two peasants? I am unable to fathom their thoughts. Anyway, the experience of free student help must be gratifying.

volume and saw that on that day in the fourth grade I had written, "I want to be a scientist in the future. I want to explore the globe for the benefit of mankind" . . .

The beach in the evening was crowded. But I quickly found Second Brother . . . Everything was ready. Then we walked about until dark and waded into the water . . . The smooth beginning gave us courage. Keeping our heads low, we swam with great caution to avoid any splashing. . . . Without incident we passed the guard post at Kulangu, not far away from Mei-mei's grave. For a moment grief over leaving her made me forget all fear, as I was carried swiftly away on the current, away from her.

We passed Kulangu and Amoy University. Looking back I saw the sky over half of Amoy Island glow red, as if it had caught fire. To our left the black hills lay stretched like an evil serpent.

Then the fear returned, and I realized that we were like two grains in the vast sea.*

More than a few of the young Red Guard leaders escaped to Taiwan. Friends there have told me of at least ten whom they know personally. Without exception, these are idealistic young people who thought they were serving their country and then became disappointed, especially when they were sent to the villages. They had been told that the villagers were happy and were living comfortable and happy lives. When they went to the villages as political cadres, they found the conditions far from what they had been led to believe, and in despair and disillusionment they had, with great difficulty and danger, escaped to Taiwan. Yet even there they had not found content. They had been too thoroughly indoctrinated with Communistic ideology. When, for example, they saw a person wearing silk or satin garments, they felt he was an enemy of the people. Thus, cut off from the past by ignorance and disappointed by the present, they despaired of the future. They are indeed a lost generation.

* Ken Ling, pp. 390–1, 394–5–6.

VIII

Has China changed in the years since I left it?

I ask myself that question many times and I search for answers. What I, and others beside me, had long foreseen was that the power of the West would decline and the power of the East would rise. Nevertheless, I had scarcely expected to see the end of the colonial era and the rise of new and independent Asian nations. That this has taken place in my lifetime I attribute to the premature decline of the West through the effect of two great world wars. The West has been all too abruptly reduced through lack of notable leaders. The most serious loss in any war is not in money or matériel or even in ordinary manpower, it is in the loss of those who, had they lived, would have been leaders, thinkers, creators. Such young men, talented, intelligent, and idealistic, are leaders wherever they are. In war as in peace they are in the forefront of action. When it is war, they lead others to battle, they take greater risks than others do, and they are killed in higher proportion. We miss

There is something touching and young today in this old country, China. I find it expressed most often in the pride with which the Chinese insist upon showing visiting foreigners their factories and machines. These places and objects, with which we are familiar in the West, are not what we go to China to see.

Nevertheless, here is a scene in Shanghai where the Chinese are making three-wheel trucks. Of course these trucks will be useful in many ways everywhere in the country, and their chief value —or perhaps menace—will be to relieve human beings of the necessity of doing certain labor. What labor will they then perform in order to live? As yet, perhaps young China has not asked the question. Perhaps the Chinese do not even realize that every machine displaces a certain number of human beings. So far, we in the West have not solved this problem, either. We are producing better and better machines while we control our population more and more efficiently.

Meanwhile China adds both people and machines to the world's problem. The woman worker in the foreground of this picture looks happy, in spite of the fact that, being only a woman, she does not get equal pay with a man. A recent Western visitor to China reports shock upon this discovery, and when he asked a young Chinese woman why her pay was less than a man's for the same work, she replied simply that men are stronger than women and deserve more pay.

them forever and to their absence from the human scene we must attribute the lack of leaders so evident among Western nations today.

In this situation it is not surprising that former colonies are struggling prematurely to organize themselves into nations, some of them colonies so long that one might say they had never been nations. The countries of Indo-China, for example, were under the power of China for a thousand years and under France for an approximate century, and now in a war situation they are struggling, inexperienced, to form their own governments.

Meantime, lack of great leaders in the West has made it impossible for the West to do anything to help a struggling Asia. We had no practical benefits to bestow on others because we ourselves were struggling under the mediocrities who were only political figures. Someone has wisely said that only great men shape great history, and today we have only events to shape history, events too great for our leaders to shape to any valuable end. Of the United States in particular the French author and scholar Amaury de Riencourt has said:

> American foreign policy was the product of American history and character: idealistic, yet unrealistic because it never seemed willing or able to relate policy with the effective power to enforce it. This was never so acutely felt as in the case of the Open Door policy, explicitly stated at the turn of the century when John Hay dispatched his notes to the world's Great Powers. The fear that China was about to be carved up by the Great Powers was not groundless, but unless the United States was prepared to back up this policy with armed strength, it was bound to remain a mere proclamation. . . . The Open Door Declaration, high-minded as it was, had unfortunate repercussions. It lured the Americans to believe that the Chinese people would be forever grateful, which of course they had no intention of being. Too many other things stood in the way: the memory of the exclusion of Chinese immigrants from the West Coast in the 1880's, the patronizing attitude which Americans share with Europeans in their dealings with Asians, the lack of psychological understanding.*

To this I would add an almost total lack of knowledge of the history

* Amaury de Riencourt, *The Soul of China*, pp. 251–2.

and culture of the individual Asian nations and peoples. Each Asian nation, each people, is different from every other. Each has its own language, costume, religion, culture, and even cuisine. I have found few Westerners, even or perhaps especially, among my own people who know this, realize it, or even care. As I write these words, I remember a night in Korea when a young man, an American and an employee of our State Department, asked for several hours alone with me. We talked far into the night and he expressed in detail his anxieties, his despair, because our preparations for helping South Korea to organize its government, its self-defense, the very life of its distracted people, were so meager, so inadequate. We knew nothing about Korea and evidently were not interested in knowing. He had been recently given special permission to attend a conference in Moscow and in Russian universities found the most thorough and careful study of Korean history, languages, and customs, preparatory to their work in North Korea and their future possible relations with all of Korea. It was from my own confirmation of his opinions that I was moved to write my long historical novel of Korea, entitled *The Living Reed,* a book for which I did an immense amount of research, although I had known Korea and Koreans all my life.

And now in China, are the Chinese themselves forgetting the past? Is the Cultural Revolution a success after all? Certainly its policy was to destroy the past, and yet as we talked that day, in Danby, Vermont, my Australian guest and I, it began to be clear to me that the past is not dead in China. Mao Tse-tung himself still uses the techniques of the past. His new ideas are expressed in old ways. Instead of reverence for ancestors he teaches reverence for the martyrs of the Revolution, who are described as benevolent and wise. Will this be enough, I wonder? I ask the question and we discuss it. A conclusion comes slowly to the surface of my mind. The greatest danger in China now is that there is no technique for succession in government. Mao Tse-tung is a great man, but where is his successor? The old techniques are gone whereby a new Emperor rose up among contenders by sheer valor. But stay— how can I be sure the contenders are not waiting, simply waiting as they used to wait, for the Emperor to die? And what is Mao Tse-tung in fact

A train trip in China is always an event, exciting in human adventure and highly educational. I have traveled thousands of miles on Chinese trains—indeed, wherever trains could travel, there went I. A book, perhaps several, could be written of my adventures on Chinese trains, some of them alarming but most of them diverting.

The trains in New China, it seems, carry on the old tradition, but not in traditional ways. For example, with Pavlovian persistence a very loud loudspeaker today drums into willing and unwilling ears alike unceasing lessons in hygiene, Maoism, patriotic songs and lectures, Maoism, agricultural techniques, Maoism, and other purposeful material. This drives the Western traveler mad until, if he is in a compartment, he can find the turn-off button. This button, however, is concealed in unexpected places and is not always found.

Service on the new trains is assiduous. The old trains were comfortably dirty. People spat on the floor and threw peanut shells and fruit pits, etc., there—indeed, where else? Windows were often hermetically sealed. Not so in the new trains, where every half hour or so an employee brushes the floor with a rice straw broom, while others serve tea or hot water, each employee serving one of these ingredients in turn. I remember, however, that even on the old trains one could order tea, also—plain or in such fancy variety as chrysanthemum tea.

The new trains, one may note with surprise, are no more democratic than the old ones. If one has the money he may travel "soft"—that is, in a four-person compartment with soft seats, pillow, sheets and blanket. Unlimited tea is provided and special dishes in the dining car. Other, less fortunate, persons sit on hard wooden seats and sleep on boards.

In fairness, however, one must say that Chinese trains today are clean, prompt and reach much farther into the country than once was the case. Even the incessant noise of the educational loudspeaker probably falls on deafened ears at last. The human capacity for not listening to what one hears is remarkable, unfailing, interracial and international.

but an Emperor? And who will say that the "young generals" will not contend again? If the last of the Red Guards are not the contenders, it may be that the young military men, seeded everywhere throughout Chinese Communist society today, will contend in the traditional fashions. To be sure, an American correspondent, recently visiting Peking, assures us that these military men are not to be confused with the warlords of the past. No? Who can tell?

And as I consider the point, has not Marx been substituted for Confucius and the formalism of Communism for the formalism of Confucianism? Confucius has today been rejected but the "thought" of Mao Tse-tung is as rigid a control as the "thought" of Confucius was for centuries. Perhaps the Chinese are not so changed, after all. Confucius controlled for many centuries after he died. That is, he controlled the conduct of life and people, until control, self-control and social control, became a people's habit. Mao Tse-tung has certainly done nothing to break the control. The "self-cultivation" so ardently preached in China nowadays is certainly very Confucian. Ah, but there is one great difference! Confucius believed in individualism; Communism teaches collectivism. Under Confucius the great individual could emerge. Can the same be true of Communism?

Meanwhile, China's efforts will be to unite its own regionalisms. In the past the provinces were separate units, loosely bound together by past history and general philosophies. Today new issues emerge. The interest centers on how the less industrialized areas can develop and on the responsibility of the more industrialized to help. The national emphasis is still on agriculture, through a reorganized system where the peasant owns his plot and takes his part in working communal land. Still, I hear that the intelligentsia disdain manual labor in spite of having to do it. It is their duty to do it and they perform their duty—but it is a shell over the old disdain.

And the arts are developing, in spite of manual labor. There is excellence developing in the modern Chinese theater, I am told—a real Chinese ballet, now that the period of imitating Russia in the 1950's is over. Old Chinese musical instruments are back again—the pí-pa, for example. They are producing operas again, sword-play, shadow-boxing, and so on, though the music is still rather Western—or Tchai-kovsky. They have not had time, perhaps, to find their own themes.

I had asked my Australian visitor how the Chinese feel toward the United States now. He replied that since the Dulles era is over, they think our two countries can cooperate. They fear Russia and Japan perhaps, the old, old fears. But there is a sort of continental affinity between the Chinese and us, as well as historical. They admire the American Revolution. They admire the fact that the United States was founded with dynamism and open-mindedness based on a true idealism. Chou En-lai speaks of this often, in contrast to the Russian point of view. Americans, he says, forget quickly and hold no grudges.

The Chinese even understand, I am told, the difficulties of our position in Vietnam and especially our predicament of wanting to leave without "loss of face." The Chinese are really not very interested in the rest of the world and have no zest for the burdens and problems of colonial power. They simply want back what was once their territory —as for example, Mongolia. They are interested in "functional techniques," and they want to get their country back to running smoothly and in good order. After all, Confucius said in effect, "Stay at home and improve yourselves"—this in contrast to Christianity, which said, "Go ye into all the world." Or, as the Australian put it, perhaps it is the chicken-and-egg business again. Did we create Christianity or did it create us?

We had wandered far and wide as we talked that day, the young Australian and I. We agreed that the China of today is still, in many ways, the China of centuries. But he made a very cogent contrast between the Mao myth, which permeates the Chinese people today, and the Confucian myth of yesterday. He said: "Confucianism was basically a way to maintain society. The Mao myth is a way to transform it."

IX

All these days I have been waiting—waiting for the letter. While I waited I have been remembering the China I knew better than I knew my own country, the people I knew better than my own. Yes, I was driven out of that country by those people, I and my family, driven out because we were foreign and white. Yet I knew the Chinese people, I knew their history, I understood, even as I was exiled, their fear of becoming a part of Western empire. They had suffered injustices. I forgave them for their ignorance of my own people. I knew how absurd and false were their accusations that Christian missionaries were spies for Western governments. I accepted their traditional ignorance of Western peoples, realizing how large China is, how old, how civilized. For I believed, knowing my parents so well and the nobility and sacrifice of their lives, that the Chinese would understand, some day, the great benefits that missionaries had brought to China. Not only the beneficence of Christian love, but the gifts of science, of modern medicine and education, the missionaries brought to China.

A Yangtse River scene, the small boats, sampans and sailboats, crowded with refugees who are returning to their homes in and about Pukow. It could be a picture from the past—the old wooden boats, seeming so untrustworthy and yet seldom wrecked or overturned, though always overloaded and overcrowded. Afar off, lofty and ignoring, a modern merchant vessel rests at dock, or if the river has silted, unloading its cargo into small boats.

So much in New China is startlingly new that one is the more surprised to find so much, also, unchanged—and perhaps unchanging. But who knows anything about China? Not even the Chinese! Each human creature knows his own tiny life and not far beyond.

. . . Oh, the memories that flash into my mind because of this letter, lying open here on my desk! . . .

I think of three American sisters, one a skilled surgeon, one an endlessly tender and patient nurse, the third a fine teacher. They lived in a remote area north of the Yangtse River in a town called Hwaiyuen, and renouncing all thought of marriage and their own homes, they devoted themselves to the Chinese people. They saved thousands of lives, those blessed women. I see their faces in my memory, the Murdock sisters, coming from a comfortable family in America to spend their lives in the heart of an alien and suspicious people ignorant of the West and unable to comprehend the Christian love that brought such missionaries to China. I remember that every morning, early, before they had eaten breakfast, they went outside the city wall to find the girl babies that Chinese families did not want and had deposited, alive, in a certain low tower called the Baby Tower and left there to die. Such as were still alive these American women took home and nurtured and saved and educated in their own school. I saw those babies grow into healthy, happy little girls and young women, to marry and become good wives and mothers. The Murdock sisters loved them all the way.

. . . The letter came this morning. I had waited weeks . . .

And why do I think of any special ones when I remember the hundreds of good Western men and women I knew during my more than forty years of life in China? I never knew one missionary, Catholic or Protestant, from America or Europe, who was not a good man or woman, their lives dedicated to helping the Chinese people. How they grieved when their own fellow citizens, traders or soldiers or diplomats, were less than just to the Chinese people! They took the side of China and protested even against their own governments. I think of the many Christian missionaries, giving their lives for the Chinese poor and oppressed, these same missionaries who were murdered, men, women and children, in the days of the Boxer Rebellion. They forgave, they understood, but they died and were left as they lay, dead.

. . . The letter—the letter is here on my desk . . .

And why do I think of this multitude of good men and women who left their homes and countries to go to faraway China and live in the midst of an alien people? Let me think of my own parents. Had they not been inspired and compelled by Christian love of all mankind, that love so strangely like the spirit of Confucius that I believe Jesus knew, five centuries later, of the great Confucius, whom today the Chinese people reject, my parents would have lived long and happily comfortable lives in their ancestral homes. They came of educated and cultivated families, gifted in the arts. My father's family was noted as linguists. My mother's family were leaders in education and creative arts. Neither family was poor. The family homes were large and comfortable.

Why did they leave all this in their youths, and against their parents' wishes go to spend their lives among and for the Chinese people?

I see my father and mother in thousands of scenes—my tall father walking up and down the floor of our living room, walking all night with his arm supporting a Chinese opium addict who had taken an overdose and must be kept awake, and my little mother brewing coffee all night to keep this Chinese awake. Who is the Chinese? I do not know—a neighbor, perhaps, whose wife came running in, weeping and imploring help. She sits weeping to one side, and I stand beside her, a child trying to comfort her.

It is one of thousands of memories. My father going off on one of his long journeys through country and village. My father at work in his study, mastering the Chinese language, translating the Greek New Testament into Chinese, the Hebrew Old Testament into Chinese. He used the Chinese vernacular decades before the literacy revolution of Hu Shih and Ch'en Tu Hsiu. His Chinese translations of the Gospels separately and then as the entire New Testament are in the museum of the American Bible Society in New York today. His unique and scholarly work on Chinese idioms is in the Library of Congress in Washington, D. C. He was a great and gifted scholar in many languages but he devoted his life to the Chinese people. He was rewarded by their love. It was his only reward and at the end of fifty-two years of noble and pure devotion to the Chinese people, whatever their class, rich and

A great holiday celebrated in Communist China is October 1, National Day. It is a day of parades, singing, dancing and explosive speeches. Anxious to show themselves patriotic in these new times, the last of the Taoist and Buddhist monks march with the Committee of Inhabitants in their city. The lotus flower, here made of paper, is a symbol of Buddhism.

Studying the faces of the monks, we see that none is very young. It is too late for these men, who have been monks since childhood, now to take up a new life, and I doubt any young Chinese would dare or care to become a monk.

poor, ignorant and learned, he died of a tropical dysentery, a Chinese disease, after three days of illness, at the age of eighty. His grave is on a mountain Kuling, in the province of Kiangsi, in China.

. . . O my beloved father, I shall never see even your grave—never, never! The letter is here, and it commands me never to return . . .

And my brave, dauntless little mother! Four children she lost, all in babyhood, all of tropical diseases. Had she stayed in her own country, in the healthful atmosphere of her beautiful ancestral home, among her loving brothers and sisters, she could have kept them alive. They died, infant martyrs, in ancient Chinese cities. They died of swift and cruel diseases for which then there was no cure. A few hours and my four-year-old sister, before I was born, died of cholera. Before I was born, my sister, aged six months, died of a sudden unknown disease, my two-year-old brother in one day of another. And when I was seven, my five-year-old brother died of diphtheria, for which in the West a cure had just been found—too late for him, in faraway China. And my beloved mother nearly died herself once of cholera, and again of tuberculosis, and at last died, too young, of tropical sprue.

Why do I suddenly remember her now, as she leaves the house, stealing out into the night, dressed in dark Chinese clothes, with only a faithful Chinese woman with her, to put a silver dollar into each of the matting huts of famine refugees from the north? She risked her life again and again for strangers in a strange land. Why, why? She was imbued with Christian love, the love that passes understanding and was never understood in China. Her grave and the graves of my little brothers and sisters are—were—in a small cemetery in Chinkiang, my Chinese home city, in Kiangsu Province. I asked recently that I be allowed to visit that city, in order that I might see my family graves. Now I know I shall never see them. Perhaps they no longer exist. Many graves have been despoiled and the bodies plowed under to fertilize the land. I shall never know. I am forbidden. I am exiled.

. . . This letter lies here. It is a menacing fist. What does it mean? The letter is written to me, but I am only one person. What does it mean to the whole world that a Chinese man, even a mere second-class official, can show such narrowness of understanding, such ignorant vindictiveness? And a whole generation of children, the beautiful Chinese children, have been brought up and are being brought up in this dangerous and vindictive ignorance! The letter makes me afraid, not for myself, for now I am old. I do not matter. The letter makes me afraid for the people of the world. It is the letter of a man ignorant of the past and the present, not only of his own country but of the world, and therefore a menace to the future of us all. Pray God he is not typical of his country or his people. Yet he is typical, I fear, of his government . . .

The memories of childhood and youth of all my life spent in China crowd about me today. My parents were unusual, perhaps, in their inheritance of intelligence. They were intellectuals, born and bred, as their children are. We are proud to be so, for every nation needs its intellectuals. Though ignorant and jealous people kill us, we are born again to emerge as leaders. A nation without intellectuals cannot live long. I am told by Chinese friends that though all children in China today have opportunities for education, only about one in ten is capable of higher education. This is a normal ratio and I believe would be valid in any country.

Those I am thinking of now, however, are not necessarily intellectuals. While it is true that once I made a public and passionate appeal for highly educated missionaries, if we are to have missionaries, at this moment I am thinking not of Western men and women, especially Americans, who carried their Christian faith to all parts of the world because they believed it their duty. I am thinking of the millions of Americans in the United States itself, who for a century and more poured out their money, the rich to build great hospitals and schools and churches in China, and the poor, our American working people, who gave of their hard-won earnings to share with the Chinese poor. In times of famine they sent food as well as money, and this for generation after generation. This I saw with my own eyes. I marvel at the generosity of American people and not only through religion. My people give extravagantly, warmly, cheerfully, to help other peoples and nations—a generosity unparalleled in human history. Certainly it is unknown in Chinese history. The missionary impulse itself was un-

This is Hangchow, in the province of Chekiang, in Central China. Everyone in the world, or everyone who knows anything about anything, knows that Hangchow is the most beautiful place in the world. Its only rival is Soochow, a little farther north. "Above is Heaven," the Chinese have said for centuries, "and on Earth are Soochow and Hangchow." More concretely, the most beautiful women in the world, they also say, come from Soochow and Hangchow.

Hangchow deserves all praise. I have been there often, enjoyed its lovely lake and excellent inns, and of course President Nixon was taken there in due course.

known in China, at least until the political implications of recent Communism have led Chinese missions to Africa and certain other small new nations. Strange that even this impulse, meager as it is, has a foreign and Western ideology behind it! Communism came into China from Russia, and Russian Communism came from Europeans such as Marx, Engels, and others. There is, however, a revolutionary spirit endemic throughout Chinese history. Again and again, peasants have rebelled, have killed intellectuals, have tried to set up a new dynasty or government, always unsuccessful until intellectuals grew old enough to control, as they always will and must.

I have a certain sympathy with this revolutionary impulse, for the intellectual elite have an obligation. They are not their own creation. Nature bestows her gifts blindly, or at least according to a chemical and mathematical formula whose structure we are only beginning dimly to surmise. So far, the brilliant brain may appear in a village and of peasant parentage—witness Mao Tse-tung, worshipped by millions, who is the son of a peasant and is himself a peasant, though an absolute ruler who has not even left his own country, except for a brief visit or two in Russia. Whether he acknowledges it or not, however, he is an intellectual and belongs to the elite. Nor is it a matter of sex. Blind Nature may give the brilliant mind even to a woman! I am amused, for an instant, to remember that Chinese Communism, or Socialism, as it prefers to be called, though it urges women to work equally with men, does not pay women the same wages. But any amusement is only for a moment.

. . . The letter—the letter! It lies there like a living snake on my desk —a poisonous snake . . .

I return to the memories that continue to emerge in their clarity out of the past. I remember that my parents taught me to respect, even to revere, the Chinese because of their great history and their ancient civilization. My Confucian Chinese tutor abetted them in his own fashion. Courtesy and mutual respect were our way of life. I never, as a child, sat in the presence of a Chinese guest. All Chinese were treated with appropriate consideration. Our servants, who were faithful and good, we treated with proper appreciation and courtesy and they stayed with us for years. In the 1927 attack upon Nanking by Communist revolutionary armies our Chinese servants were loyal to us. One woman, a strong peasant who risked her life for us, somehow even found her way to Unzen, Japan, where we had fled for refuge, after our homes were destroyed and all our possessions seized.

One morning, I remember, in our lonely little Japanese house on a hillside, I heard a knock at the door. It was seven o'clock, I remember, and I was bestirring myself to get some sort of breakfast for the children, my only kitchen and stove a small charcoal brazier. I supposed, hearing the knock at the door, that it was the old village woman who came often in the early morning up the mountain to sell us fresh crabs from the seashore below. Instead it was Ch'u Sau-tse, one of our Chinese servants.

I gasped aloud. "How did you get here? How did you find us?"

"You need me," she said briskly.

In she came, her belongings in a bundle, and swept me away.

"I will do everything," she announced.

And so proceeded to do, and even now, remembering her robust frame and round, rosy face, I put down my pen to laugh, though that morning is decades away, and I am here in Vermont at my desk on a bright May morning, a bed of tulips glittering scarlet and gold on the hill outside my window. Yet, remembering, I feel the old love for the Chinese people I have known as I have known no others, and whom I love today as ever, although among them were those who sought to kill me and mine.

. . . Yes, even though this letter threatens me now and refuses to allow my return to the country where I have lived most of my life and where, in my own fashion, I do live still, and shall forever . . .

It is of course inevitable that my whole being and personality are shaped by my childhood and youth in China. My parents made their friends among the Chinese almost exclusively. My father, an unbending and somewhat formal man, found his friends among Chinese scholars and intellectuals. My mother's personal friends were of the same caliber, but she was warmhearted and as quick to sympathize with a farmer's wife or a famine refugee as she did with the ladies in a wealthy family. All were human beings and, since we lived in a Chinese community, Chinese human beings. Nevertheless, we were intellectuals and our closest friends were Chinese intellectuals and therefore the elite. This helps me to understand the plight of the intellectual elite in the present revolution in China now.

I understood as well the life and grievances of the Chinese peasants. For since the special gifts that Nature bestows so indiscriminately are given without any aid or even deserving on our part, we who have been given such gifts have an obligation to use those gifts for the benefit of all and not only for ourselves or our kind. This my parents impressed upon me and therefore we received a peasant with the same welcome that we received any friend. All were our friends.

I had the privilege of knowing and to some degree sharing the life of peasants, by the chance that my mother did not enjoy living in the great provincial capital, Chinkiang, and therefore we built our home on a low hill outside the city. There were many such hills in our countryside and in the valleys were fertile farms, small but beautifully managed. Since I was an only child for a long time, after the many deaths in our family, I ran down our hill every day after my lessons and played with peasant children, knew their families and circumstances, shared their meals often, and urged the children to come and play with me after their work, too. Later, after my marriage, I lived in peasant country in the northern part of Anhwei province, and again shared the peasants' lives in various ways. I knew them well, therefore, and over many years. I know them now.

When, after college, I returned to China, prepared to spend my life there, I rejoined my old friends among the young Chinese intellectuals. We discussed everything under Heaven, but mainly we discussed the new literature and what part we, as writers and creative persons, could and should take in it. My friends, some of them, were writing imitatively after the fashion of Western writers, and I argued that there was a whole new area of wonderful life material among our own Chinese peasants. I found my suggestions coolly received. Who, they retorted, could be interested in Chinese peasants?

"I am," I replied.

Thereupon I set myself to my own writing and beginning with *The Good Earth,* I wrote a series of novels.

Later, of course, many good Chinese writers wrote on peasant subjects. Lu Hsün was very famous; so too were Ting Ling and my special friend Lao Shê. I saw him last on a visit in my Pennsylvania home and we discussed for hours his return to Peking, where his home was, and whither he longed to return, though by that time we both knew it would be dangerous for him unless he could declare himself a Communist.

Ah, that visit! During a weekend I gave a big party in our huge old Pennsylvania barn. It was a very special party. The surgeon at the Veterans' Hospital in Valley Forge had asked me to give it for a large group of veterans who were recovering from plastic surgery on their faces. They were victims of the booby traps of the Second World War, and they had lost or damaged the lower parts of their faces. Though the surgery was proceeding well, the men were timid about appearing in public, and this party was to be a first appearance for them. All went well, I might say, but Lao Shê endeared himself to us by his performance of shadow boxing, at which he was adept—so adept, indeed, that it appeared as a beautiful dance, a *pas de seul.*

More than ever, I dreaded to have him leave us. Homesickness, however, was too strong, and he returned, to be welcomed, as a matter of fact, and given a high position in Peking. But he was a great writer above all else, not an administrator or politician. I surmise all this; I told him not to write to me, for his own safety, since at that time the United States was not in favor with the new Chinese government. Others told me of him, nevertheless, and eventually the inevitable happened. He could not live under political controls, as no creative writer can, to the great loss of a nation, and he committed suicide.

. . . The letter here on my desk reminds me of his death. These ignorant, narrow, political controls end the freedom in which alone a creative mind and spirit can give his gifts to his country and the world . . .

The devotion of my parents to their work and the conscientious teaching of my Confucian Chinese tutor shaped not only my lifestyle, but, as I said, my entire personality. I grew up with a sense of joyous

A very good glimpse, here, of a modern street in Peking. It is Chang-an Avenue, and the street leading into it is Wang Fu-jing Da Jieh, according to the Chinese characters on the sign to the right. Since I see no characters for the avenue, and only happen to know its name, I do not know whether the translation of the Long Peace would be correct. If by chance it is indeed the Avenue of Long Peace, it would be—amusing? suitable? ironic?—for we see a platoon of soldiers in winter uniform marching along more or less side by side.

The large modern building is of the blocklike modern Russian type and I remember that it caused great grief to a talented young Chinese architect I know—educated in the United States, who returned to his country for patriotic reasons, hoping to have a part in creating modern buildings based on beautiful Chinese architecture. Alas, he was ignored, as were so many gifted young American-educated Chinese—nuclear scientists excepted—and now he lives in another country, self-exiled.

As for me, I like to see on Chang-an Avenue the many bicycles instead of the former man-pulled rickshas, and I especially like the determined small figure, apparently alone but with purposeful stride, as he—or she—enters, hooded against the cold Peking wind, at the extreme lower right-hand corner of the scene. He is the Chinese of the future, and I suspect—it is a mere suspicion, of course—that he is going at cross-purposes with the crowd.

obligation. I was never a missionary, although at times I taught, as a young woman, in missionary as well as in Chinese government universities. No, the obligation was to fulfill my own talents, such as they were and are, and since at that time I knew little of any people except the Chinese, it was natural, as well as my desire, to write in English about the Chinese people. And incidentally, or so I dreamed, my books might help my American people better to understand my Chinese people. I say incidentally, for I am not a missionary even in spirit. I am careful to make my books accurate to the facts as I know them, but I have no sense of mission. Since I had lived all my life in China, my material was Chinese, until I could include my own country and, to a lesser degree, elsewhere. My books are written out of life where I live it.

. . . The letter, here on my desk, is written by someone who has never read any of my books. Perhaps he has read only *The Little Red Book*. I have read it, too. It made me want to weep to think it is the only book that many Chinese are given to read. Their own great literature, and all the literature of the many countries of the world, remains beyond their reach or even their knowledge. And the young writers, their talents prohibited—alas, my beloved land, China! In what poverty you live today! . . .

But I comfort myself. It has all happened before. It will change, as it has always changed. Fifty years of a foreign-inspired Communism —what are they in comparison to five thousand years of Chinese life? Nevertheless, for the moment, the letter stares me in the face. Then I laugh. In the face, yes—but it does not reach my heart! I am in a free country, my own country, and I am free, I am free! Yesterday on a special occasion I was presented with a gift from the President of the United States. His daughter made the presentation of the gift, since he is in Russia, but it was bought on his recent visit to the New China, as a sample of the work being done there. When I opened it, I found it was a nest of lacquer boxes, each growing smaller and smaller, one within the other. I am sure the gift was not chosen with any idea of symbolism. But for me as a creative writer, there is a profound symbolism here: a box imprisoning box after box, each with its lid, until the last one is so tiny that it can contain—what? Nothing! I laugh!

. . . What has this to do with the letter? There is a symbolism. Control—control—control—until at last, nothing! . . .

I live in a free country. I know it is free. Yes, freedom brings problems, but we can solve them because we are free to do so, we, the people. We suffer for our mistakes but they are *our* mistakes, not the mistakes of autocratic rulers. We are free to work. We are even free not to work.

How narrowly I escaped! For I was very reluctant to leave China forever and come to a country strange to me, even though I knew it was my own. Had it not been for the narrow doctrine of Communism which I saw crystallizing into control, I would have taken a chance. I would have stayed in China. I might even have given up my American citizenship as my friend Edgar Snow did, in order that he might go freely to China.

I confess that when I got a letter from Chou En-lai in 1943, a brief letter asking me to come back to China and see what the Eighth Route Army was doing, I was tempted. Had it not been a foreign Communism that was using the Eighth Route Army, I might have accepted the invitation. I have that letter still. I referred to it when I wrote to Chou En-lai recently, as Premier of the People's Republic of China, saying that now, since our President's visit, I would like to see for myself the "new" China, in order that I might help, by my books yet to be written, the new upspring of friendship between our two peoples.

I received no reply. Knowing well the habitual courtesy of the China of the past, I was at least surprised. An American friend who knows this new China well, however—in fact, he went to China before President Nixon went—told me that the present-day Chinese "never answer letters." Well, each generation, each era, has its own ways and manners. Courtesy is not inherited. It must be taught.

. . . This discourteous letter, lying open before me, is an attack, not a letter. It is violent, it is uninformed, it is untruthful. Obviously the writer, a minor official in a minor post, has not read my books. None of my books is to be found in China today, although they were widely translated and read in the China I knew. When *The Good Earth* appeared in China in 1933 more than twenty different translations were made. They were all pirated, of course, and some bore only the translator's name. I did not mind, so long as my readers enjoyed the book.

"My only criticism of this book," a famous Chinese writer said, "is that it should have been written by a Chinese." . . .

I see that I am trying to comfort myself for the brutality of this letter from New China. I will stop. There is no comfort necessary—only pity. Pity the people! Do they know their own glorious history? Is their inheritance forgotten in these days of a new foreign imperialism? The tragedy of the Red Guard Cultural Revolution was—and is and forever will be—that ignorant rulers ordered the young Chinese, this generation, to destroy their own magnificent inheritance. The glory of China is her own civilization wrought by thousands of years of their own history. The gravest sin of the present is to reject, even destroy, the past, for not only the present generation is robbed, but all future generations. Yet this happened, to the horror of a watching world! How ignorant those rulers! Pity the innocent young who obeyed such commands!

If this is true—and I shall not be able to see for myself, the letter forbids me—then what is left to the Chinese people except this new political doctrine, this foreign imperialism called Communism or Socialism?

Yet let me be just. A change was inevitable. The Manchu dynasty had ended. Christian schools had brought to Chinese students Western ideas of modern times, as I have said, and young revolutionaries seized upon these ideas as later they seized upon Communism from Russia. But the gravest danger of all lay in the hopeless separation between the peasant and the indifferent and callous-hearted intellectual elite. This above all gave the peasant leader Mao Tse-tung the fuel for the dangerous fire he lit. He delivered his people to a strange and alien system, yet a system which, as I have said before, had been tried and had failed in earlier times, even in China. The new generation has been denied the knowledge of the history of their own civilization. They can only parrot the cries of a new and unproved political system.

. . . The letter brings me back to its vicious attack. Sir, you the writer, the second secretary in the Chinese embassy in another country, I know Communism in China! I know well of what I have written. I have seen for myself. Your letter lies. Or perhaps it is only that you are ignorant. You have not been allowed to read my books. You repeat only what you have been taught and told to say. It is all you know . . .

Yet I will be just. Every people has the right to choose its own government although any government is only as good as its administrators. The Chinese people have a right to be Communist, Socialist, whatever they please. They will learn by hard experience, and experience will teach them to choose what finally will be. And there is good in this New China. I am told that all the people are fed. There is food for everyone. Those who rule feast, of course, but that is to be expected. This does not matter if the people are fed.

And there are schools for all. That, too, is good. Everyone now has the opportunity to learn to read and write. Chin Shih Huang, who united China into one country, one nation, about the time the Christian era began, was afraid of intellectuals and killed them. Then he became fearful of books, for books influence the minds of people and create subversive and original thought. Therefore he ordered books to be burned. The New China has reversed the tyranny. The people are taught to read, but what they read is rigidly controlled. Writers, too, are rigidly controlled. My books, for example, unimportant as they may be, are nowhere to be found in China today, although they are in other Communist countries and are read with apparent enjoyment, if I am to judge by sales reports. But in China? They touch a sore spot there, somehow. Perhaps they are too factual. I was trained by my scholar father. I do sound research before I write. I do not write before I know my facts.

When I write my next novel, therefore, it will be about China and it will be built upon solid foundations of fact. True, I shall not have been in Red China. But I have my friends, my many trustworthy Chinese

The landscapes of Kweilin province are carved by the winds and rains of centuries. Here are the mountains beloved by Chinese artists. Ancient paintings portray these peaks, wreathed in mist. They are almost cliffs and do indeed break frequently into insurmountable rock.

In the midst of this somber and spectacular scenery the Chinese pursues the ways of his ancestors. Here rice seedlings are being transplanted into flooded fields, a sight so familiar to me from my Chinese childhood that I never see it, even in photographs, without a pang of nostalgic memory. The season was always early June —and daily I ran down the hill on which we lived to join the peasants in the valley. It was a season of hard work but of hope. The planting of rice! It was a preparation for the harvest of plenty.

friends, those who visit me in secret. That is hard to bear. Why must we meet in secret? Because they live in fear!

I visited for myself, recently, the "new Chinese" in New York, the ones who form the Chinese delegation to the United Nations. It was an interesting experience. I had an appointment, of course. I arrived promptly, accompanied by my business manager. The building is not an embassy, for diplomatic relations have not, as yet, proceeded that far. It was, in fact, a motel and it still looks like a motel. The first floor has been cleared into a large lobby with various small enclaves.

A young man sauntered toward us, wearing a gray cotton pajama suit. We announced our appointment and he repeated it in a loud voice to various young men loitering about. We sat down and waited and the young man sat down and stared at us, knees crossed and foot swinging. I wore my usual costume, a long Chinese robe of brocaded satin. He stared at it.

"This old fashion," he said in broken English.

I agreed. "Yes, I am very old-fashioned."

He stared, laughed, and remarked in Chinese to other young men who came to stare at us that I was old-fashioned. I understood, of course, but I had been warned by Chinese friends that I must use only English if I went to China. This in a sense was also China, and so I looked vacant.

In truth, however, I was deeply interested in all I saw and heard. This was indeed "new China." That is, it would have been impossible to meet such young men in so important a place in old China. I had known Hu Shih well when he was Ambassador to the United States. I had been in and out of official Chinese buildings in various parts of the world. Quiet, a trained and courteous staff, respect and decorum, all were there. And beauty was there in decorations of art and flowers and tea served hot and immediate.

Here, all was confusion and yet idleness. No one was busy, there was total lack of order. Curiously, I felt no ill will in the atmosphere, only curiosity and crudity. I had met both often enough in remote villages in China where no one had ever seen a foreigner. Not imagining they could be understood, they had expressed there, as here, their naïve comments, their wonder.

After some time we were taken upstairs to the Personage we had come to see. She was dressed in the same drab cotton pajamalike garments the young men wore downstairs. Four red plastic covered armchairs were set about a low, round table. There were no decorations of any kind. The walls were bare. This I excused because the building had only recently been bought. Tea was served by a careless young man, and another like him slapped a pile of propaganda magazines on the table. Both departed.

The Personage obviously did not know how to proceed. In deference I waited. She spoke a halting but correct English.

"You—speak—Chinese?" she asked.

Remembering advice, I replied in English that I had been speaking English for many years.

She handed us the magazines. "Please—take—to read carefully."

I accepted them.

"You—wish—to go—China?" she asked.

"Very much," I replied. "I lived there for more than forty years. I was taken there as an infant by my parents and grew up there. Now I hear of much that is new. I would like to see for myself all that is being done for the people."

"We—here—cannot decide," she said. "Peking—decides—everything."

"I have been told that," I replied. "But I am in a quandary. I have promised to go on the 'Voice of America' this afternoon. What I say will be broadcast all over the world. I am certain that I shall be asked if I am visiting China. What shall I say? I am here to ask your advice."

She pondered this for a long time, her straight hair, not quite shoulder-length, falling over her face. Then she replied:

"Only—Peking—decides. We can—decide nothing—here. Nothing —only Peking."

"I understand that very well," I replied. "Shall I say that?"

She pondered again. At last she said with some resolution, looking at me for the first time, "I—think—you may say—you will—visit China, but—not when."

"Thank you," I replied. "I shall follow your advice."

There was nothing more to be said, it seemed. No one had touched the tea. I rose and she rose. She pointed to the magazines.

"Please—study—carefully," she urged again.

"I will," I promised.

I had not the heart to tell her I had, of course, already seen the magazines and had read them. From somewhere they are mailed to me regularly. Yet she was courteous to me in her fashion. She accompanied me in the elevator down to the first floor again and then to the door. Young men in the same drab garb were still wandering aimlessly about, laughing, talking, smoking cigarettes, reading newspapers. At the door the Personage and I stopped. What is correct in New China? Does one bow as we used to do in old China? She did not bow, and therefore I did not. We merely parted. Outside it was raining and I hurried to my waiting car.

Looking back on that strange, unlovely visit, I remember that the only brightening of the woman's plain face was an instant when she spoke of Hangchow, her native town, when I asked from what part of China she came. We agreed on its beauty. Hangchow has been famous for centuries. My parents went their upon their first arrival in China, in 1880. That is now almost a century ago! But the natural beauty of Hangchow is deathless.

When I told a Chinese friend of my visit to the Personage he said, "She is very highly thought of in Peking." Looking back upon my visit, I am glad I went. I understand now that peasants and the children of peasants are trying to learn how to be rulers instead of always the ruled. No wonder they seek for modern patterns. I am sorry for them. The task is monumental. The largest population in the world, the next-to-largest land mass, the oldest history, a modern life-style foreign to them but complete with modern nuclear weapons—how can one feel less than pity for the Chinese people today? Time is what they need, time and isolation. But there is no time and there can be no isolation any more, not for China or for any country.

This letter on my desk—I wonder if Chou En-lai himself is behind it? It is more than possible. He forgets nothing, this man. He is a relentless ruler behind all his brilliance and suavity. Of course he is the real ruler in China today. And of course he remembers his invitation to me in 1943 to give up my own country and return to a Communist China. It was an argument I had often with my old friend Edgar Snow. I knew him in China, where he visited me in my Chinese home. I knew him later in the United States, where he visited me in my Pennsylvania house. My children were small then, and I remember a great argument I had with Edgar Snow one bright summer morning out under the big black walnut tree. A swing hangs there and my youngest son, at that time three years old, was swinging, I giving him a push now and then.

"You will have to choose between Communist China and your own country one of these days," I warned Edgar Snow.

"I haven't much choice then," he told me. "I'm a journalist and the news will be in China as long as I live."

Eventually he did indeed give up his country. He moved to Switzerland and came and went freely to China. It was ironic and sad that he died of cancer in Switzerland just before President Nixon visited Peking. Edgar Snow's widow, her sister and son, were welcomed in Peking recently and Chou En-lai talked long and privately with her, she reported.

As for me, I chose my own country. Unlike Edgar Snow, I had grown up in China and had lived there half my life. I knew very little about my own people and very much about the Chinese. If I had a professional motive as a writer, it was to help my people understand the Chinese whom I knew so well. I had been educated thoroughly in Chinese history, literature, and arts. I spoke Chinese before I spoke English. I had lived through the revolutionary years in China. I foresaw the future clearly. It was the Americans who needed to know and understand the Chinese.

"I must choose my own country," I told Edgar Snow that summer's day. "Americans need me more now than the Chinese do." We went our separate directions thereafter and seldom met.

I have never regretted my decision to stay with my own country. I believe in our form of government. It is truly a people's government based on great human ideals. It fails when we, as human beings, fail. When we achieve, our government is the greater. Above all, our government is based on the freedom of the individual. In complete freedom I have lived where I pleased, as I pleased, and I have written as I pleased. I am not degraded or punished because I am an intellectual by heritage or choice. I am free to develop myself. I am proud to be an American. This is not to say that ours is the best country in the world. It *is* to say that for me it is the best country.

. . . Somehow, while I have been writing these pages, the sting has gone out of the letter. I do not care any more. The wound is healed, the discourtesy ignored. Therefore, I am able now to quote the letter as it is, as it has been, lying before me on my desk, these several days. This is the letter:

May 17, 1972.

Dear Miss Pearl Buck,

Your letters have been duly received.

In view of the fact that for a long time you have in your works taken an attitude of distortion, smear and vilification towards the people of new China and their leaders, I am authorized to inform you that we can not accept your request for a visit to China.

Sincerely yours

(H. L. Yuan)
Second Secretary

L'Envoi

O my dear people of China! Dear because of all my childhood in China, all my Chinese friends through all my youth and young womanhood, even until half my life was spent! I speak as your life-long friend.

You have much to endure before your future is clear and peaceful. When this Emperor dies, this Mao Tse-tung, there will be wars among you as there have always been when an Emperor dies and there is no heir to take his place. There will be a struggle in all your members, a regional struggle, until the new Emperor appears. And the struggle for his emergence will be, as it has always been, among the young generals. They are waiting in every province in your country, their armies trained and poised, each army loyal to its own general, and only to him. The victor in this struggle will be your new Emperor, whether you call him that or not. His will be "the mandate of Heaven," because what you, the people of China, want is always the mandate of Heaven.

This is a study in faces, Chinese faces in a modern China. Foremost in the scene are two elderly men. One wears the traditional long gown of the old-fashioned Chinese gentleman. He wears, too, an old-fashioned cap, he carries a cane. He is a man of substance. He is firm of face, determined, unbending, unheeding of the young people pushing their way behind him.

By whatever name you call yourselves, you are still the People of the Middle Kingdom, the Center of the World.

I shall never see you again, nor will you see me. It has been forbidden us. You will smile, perhaps, when I tell you that although I have been many times invited to visit Taiwan, I have never accepted, lest your rulers take it as a political act and forbid me a visit to you on the mainland. But this does not matter now. Already the son of President Chiang is negotiating the return of Taiwan to China. This is, of course, inevitable, whether the people of Taiwan wish it or not.

No, I shall never see you again, my beloved people of China. My feet will never again tread the hills, the villages, the cities I know so well. Yet, though this is true, it, too, no longer matters to me. Whether you even want me to come back to you no longer matters to me. I am a part of you forever, as you are of me. You formed me, you fed me, you shaped me as I am forever.

A part of me remains eternally with you. My parents lie in your earth. They spent their lives with you and for you. In death they are with you still. With them are also my two brothers and two sisters who died in childhood of diseases endemic in your country. They never saw America, their ancestral land. They are forever a part of China, as I am also, save that I still live and am safely in my native land, for here I, the only one of seven children, was born.

Here, too, in freedom, I have done my work. I have steadfastly helped my American people to understand, respect, and even love you, my Chinese people. I have had my part in our President's visit to Peking, for our people wished him to go. They do not feel you are strangers, whatever the difference in our governments. I am proud to know that through my writings I have helped to create and sustain this feeling. I shall continue to do so.

All that China gave me, the friendships, the beauty, the excitement, the dangers—yes, there were dangers to my very life and the lives of my family and we were saved by our Chinese friends—all my experiences for so many years, I have poured into my books. My books have taken me, and you with me, far and wide upon our Earth. I am glad for your sake that I am the most widely translated author my country has ever had, for that means that you, too, are also widely known. To the best of my ability, I have tried to speak for you. I was proud that the Nobel Prize for Literature was awarded to me for "rich and genuine epic portrayals of Chinese peasant life."

I was humbly happy that my parents were also mentioned in the added phrase, "and for masterpieces of biography." For in their time my father and mother obeyed the mandate of Heaven as it was given to them: "Go ye into all the world!"

In my own way, in my own time, I too have obeyed the mandate of Heaven. For me it is expressed through the words of eternal truth spoken by Confucius, who yet lives, though he was born five hundred years before the Christian era.

"Under Heaven," he said, "All Are One."

Danby House
Danby, Vermont
May 30, 1972